MEETING

St. Matthew

TODAY

D1596447

MEETING

St. Matthew

TODAY

Understanding the Man,
His Mission, and His Message

DANIEL J. HARRINGTON, SJ

LOYOLA PRESS.
A JESUIT MINISTRY
Chicago

LOYOLA PRESS.
A JESUIT MINISTRY

3441 N. Ashland Avenue
Chicago, Illinois 60657
(800) 621-1008
www.loyolapress.com

Cover image: Saint Matthew, illustration for 'The Life of Christ', c.1886–94 (w/c & gouache on paperboard), Tissot, James Jacques Joseph (1836-1902) / Brooklyn Museum of Art, New York, USA / The Bridgeman Art Library
Cover design by Kathryn Seckman Kirsch
Interior design by Kathryn Seckman Kirsch and Joan Bledig

Library of Congress Cataloging-in-Publication Data
Harrington, Daniel J.
    Meeting St. Matthew today / Daniel J. Harrington
        p. cm.
    Includes Bibliographical references (p.   ).
    ISBN-13: 978-0-8294-2914-5
    ISBN-10: 0-8294-2914-X
    1. Bible. N.T. Matthew—Commentaries. I. Title. II. Title: Meeting St. Matthew today.
    BS2575.53.H373 2010
    226.2'06—dc22
                                                      2010020510

Printed in the United States of America
10 11 12 13 14 15 Versa 10 9 8 7 6 5 4 3 2 1

Contents

A Year Dedicated to Matthew the Evangelist...................... vii

Part One: Meeting St. Matthew

1 The Evangelist and His Gospel..........................3

Part Two: Matthew's Story of Jesus

2 Jesus' Origins and Beginnings: Matthew 1—4.............. 15

3 Jesus Is Powerful in Word and Deed: Matthew 5—9.....25

4 Jesus' Mission: Acceptance and Rejection:
Matthew 10—12..35

5 The Kingdom of God and the Suffering Messiah:
Matthew 13—17...45

6 Jesus' Way to Jerusalem: Matthew 18—23....................57

7 Jesus' Final Discourse and His Death and
Resurrection: Matthew 24—28........................... 71

**Part Three: Distinctive Features of
Matthew's Gospel**

8 A Jewish Book..87

9 A Christian Gospel 99

Part Four: Matthew's Gospel in Christian Life

10 Preaching and Teaching This Gospel 111

Readings from Matthew's Gospel for the Sundays
and Feasts in the Year A 129

For Further Reading 131

About the Author 133

A Year Dedicated to Matthew the Evangelist

Matthew's Gospel is best known for the Magi story, the Sermon on the Mount, the Last Judgment scene ("the sheep and the goats"), and the risen Jesus' command to "make disciples of all nations." Jesus is portrayed as the great teacher, and many of his teachings featured in Matthew have strongly influenced Christian theology and practice throughout history.

In the Year A (2011, 2014, 2017, 2020, 2023, etc.) in the Catholic Church's lectionary of Scripture readings for Mass, the Gospel passage almost every Sunday is taken from St. Matthew. In the New Testament we meet St. Matthew only indirectly through the Gospel that bears his name. Matthew's Gospel is one of the longest books in the New Testament and has exercised great influence in Christian life over the centuries. It has even been called the most important book ever written.

On the one hand Matthew's Gospel is often described as the most Jewish Gospel, and on the other hand Matthew is sometimes accused of being anti-Jewish. How to resolve and explain this apparent contradiction has been one of my special concerns as a biblical scholar. I'm convinced that we can understand the paradox of Matthew's Gospel best when we place it in its historical context in late first-century Judaism.

After a brief introduction to what can be said with confidence about the author of this Gospel, this volume provides in six chapters a narrative analysis of the entire Gospel. These chapters focus on the Gospel's key words and images, characters, plot, literary forms, indications of time and place, and theological message. The next two chapters treat its place within late first-century Judaism (as a "Jewish book") and the Gospel's major theological themes (as a "Christian Gospel"). The final chapter offers suggestions for preachers, teachers, and all who love Scripture about how Matthew's Gospel might be used more effectively in the church today. Questions for reflection and discussion are provided in each chapter, and the volume can be used easily by Bible study groups.

It has been my privilege to teach many courses on Matthew's Gospel and to write a large commentary and many articles about it. This Gospel corresponds nicely to my two great interests as a biblical scholar: Judaism in Jesus' time, and the New Testament. My full-scale commentary *The Gospel of Matthew* was the first volume published in the Sacra Pagina series (Liturgical Press, 1991), and has been reprinted (with an updated bibliography) in a paperback edition (2007). I am grateful to Loyola Press for the invitation to synthesize my views on Matthew's Gospel and present them to a wider audience.

PART ONE

Meeting St. Matthew

1

The Evangelist and His Gospel

We know St. Matthew principally (if not entirely) from the Gospel that traditionally bears his name. The Evangelist seems to have been Jewish in his background and interests. He delights in showing how Jesus fulfills Israel's Scriptures. He not only quotes several biblical passages explicitly but also provides many allusions to and echoes of Scripture. The many ethical teachings of Jesus that this Gospel writer conveys were at home in first-century Judaism and are reflected in the later rabbinic writings. Matthew stands in opposition to certain other Jews whom he calls "hypocrites" and who control "their synagogues." He is especially concerned to portray Jesus as the authoritative interpreter of the Mosaic Law (Torah) and one who opposes the interpretations of it put forward by the scribes and Pharisees. Matthew's major theological themes (kingdom of heaven, righteousness, eschatology) and titles for Jesus (Messiah, Son of David, Son of Man, Son of God, Lord) have deep Jewish roots.

And yet nowhere in the Gospel does the Evangelist identify himself by name or claim to be an eyewitness. The title "According to Matthew" seems to have been added in the second century when the connection was made between this Gospel and Matthew the tax collector, who became one of the twelve apostles. This ascription raises more questions than it answers. Why was this same tax collector called Levi the son of Alphaeus in Mark 2:14? Where did a tax collector get such an extensive Jewish education as this Evangelist clearly received? Why did he rely on written sources such as Mark's Gospel and the Sayings Source Q in writing his own Gospel? But even if the traditional ascription is dubious, why then was this Gospel associated with Matthew the tax collector? Had he done missionary work in the area in which the Gospel was composed? Was he regarded as that community's patron saint? Was he responsible for handing on some of the special traditions found only in this Gospel? Scholars have wrestled with these questions for centuries. For our purposes it is enough to refer to the Evangelist behind this Gospel as "Matthew" and to try to learn as much as we can about him from a careful reading of the text that has borne his name for many centuries.

The community in which and for which Matthew originally wrote appears to have been predominantly (if not exclusively) made up of Jewish Christians. The Evangelist assumes that they keep the Jewish Law as interpreted by Jesus (5:17–20) and observe the Sabbath rest (12:1–14; 24:20). He has no need to explain to them the Jewish practices of ritual purity (15:2) and the customs of wearing prayer shawls and phylacteries (23:5). He situates Jesus' views on marriage and divorce in the context of contemporary Jewish debates about the grounds on which a Jewish man might divorce his wife (5:32; 19:9). During his earthly ministry Matthew's Jesus insists that he has been sent "only to the lost sheep of the house of Israel" (15:24; see 10:5–6), and only after his resurrection does he send his disciples to "all nations" (28:19).

From what we can learn about the Evangelist and the community for which he wrote, it seems fair to describe this Gospel as the most Jewish of the four Gospels. This is probably why it eventually was placed first in the New Testament—because it provides the perfect bridge between the Old and the New Testaments. However, it soon circulated in Christian communities throughout the Mediterranean world, became a Gospel for all Christians, and has exercised such enormous influence throughout the centuries that it has been called the most important book ever written.

On the basis of possible allusions to Matthew's Gospel in 1 and 2 Peter and in early patristic writings (*Didache*, the letters of Ignatius), it appears that Matthew's Gospel was composed before A.D. 100. The earliest date would be around A.D. 70, since there seem to be references to the destruction of Jerusalem that occurred then (21:41; 22:7; 27:25). These allusions plus the Evangelist's use of Mark's Gospel (which was written around A.D. 70) indicate that this Gospel was composed around A.D. 85 or 90.

The Jewish character of Matthew's Gospel suggests a place of composition in the eastern Mediterranean area. It must have been a city where Greek was spoken and read, with a large Jewish population and a substantial Jewish Christian community. The best candidate is Antioch in Syria, though Caesarea Maritima in Palestine and Damascus in Syria are also possible.

Matthew set out to produce a revised and expanded version of Mark's Gospel. As a careful editor, Matthew often corrected and improved Mark's Greek and omitted what apparently he considered unnecessary details. He also wanted to include more of Jesus' teachings that were available to him (and to Luke also) through what modern scholars have designated as the Sayings Source Q, as well as the many other traditions unique to this Gospel and now designated as M (for Matthew). This Evangelist has been correctly described as both a transmitter and an interpreter of traditions. While most of his material was already traditional by his time, Matthew edited it and gave it a distinctive shape in order to address the historical crisis that all Jews experienced after the destruction of Jerusalem and its temple in A.D. 70.

The three great pillars of Judaism in Jesus' time were the Jerusalem temple, the land of Israel, and the Mosaic Law (Torah). But after the disastrous Jewish revolt of A.D. 66–73, the temple and the city were in ruins, and the land was even more firmly under Roman control than before. And so all Jews had to face the question, How best can the Jewish heritage be rescued and preserved? Some Jews (Zealots) prepared for another military rebellion. Others (apocalyptists) looked for divine intervention in the near future, while faithfully observing the Torah in the present. Still others (scribes and Pharisees, the forerunners of the rabbis) gathered the traditions surrounding the Torah in order to make possible a more perfect observance of it. In this context Matthew put forward Jesus of Nazareth as the authoritative interpreter of the Torah, and the movement gathered around him as the best way of carrying on Israel's heritage as God's people. Matthew sought to address the new situation and the new questions that had arisen for Jewish Christians like himself in the late first century. He did so by emphasizing Jesus' place in the Jewish tradition and community.

Matthew's Gospel is a revised and expanded version of Mark's Gospel. Almost everything in the sixteen chapters of Mark is included, though often in a somewhat compressed form. In the first twelve chapters Matthew does not follow Mark's sequence very closely. But from chapter 13 onward he is more careful in observing Mark's outline. On the whole, his geographical outline is taken from Mark. After movements in various places are described in 1:1—4:11, the Matthean Jesus exercises his ministry in Galilee (4:12—13:58), around Galilee and on the way to Jerusalem (14:1—20:34), and in Jerusalem (21:1—28:20). To Mark's outline Matthew has added the infancy narrative in chapters 1 and 2 and the climactic appearance of the risen Jesus in chapter 28.

Matthew has also greatly expanded the teaching material found in Mark through the inclusion of many sayings found in the Q source and in traditions special to Matthew. He has shaped these materials into five great speeches: the Sermon on the Mount, the Missionary Discourse, the Parables of the Kingdom, the Advice to the Community, and the Eschatological Discourse. For each block of teaching, Matthew has furnished a narrative introduction and a formula marking the conclusion: "when Jesus had finished saying these things . . ." According to Matthew, Jesus was and is the wisest teacher of all because he is also the Son of God (see 11:25–30).

Between the speeches, Matthew provides short narratives or stories, which in their own way serve as vehicles for the wisdom of Jesus. Matthew even turns the miracle stories into encounters with Jesus and examples of "praying faith." Also, certain key words and phrases ("pay homage" or "worship," "righteousness," "little faith") move the plot along and provide a sense of unity to the overall story. All these elements combine to produce the following outline of Matthew's Gospel:

- The "who" and "where" of Jesus (1:1—2:23)
- The beginning of Jesus' activity (3:1—4:25)
- The Sermon on the Mount (5:1—7:29)
- Jesus' powerful deeds (8:1—9:38)
- The missionary discourse (10:1–42)
- The rejection of Jesus (11:1—12:50)
- The parables of the kingdom (13:1–53)
- Miracles, controversies, and the cross (13:54—17:27)
- Advice to the community (18:1–35)
- More opposition to Jesus (19:1—23:39)
- The eschatological discourse (24:1—25:46)
- Jesus' passion, death, and resurrection (26:1—28:20)

While Matthew may well be the most Jewish Gospel, for some it is also the most anti-Jewish. Its emphasis on Jesus as the fulfillment of the Old Testament and as the authoritative interpreter of the Torah can give the impression to some that the Jewish tradition has been exhausted and is no longer meaningful. It also contains a blistering attack on the scribes and Pharisees as hypocrites in chapter 23, and throughout keeps up a polemic against "their synagogues." In 27:25 we are told that in response to Pilate's wavering over whether to have Jesus executed "the people as a whole answered, 'His blood be on us and on our children!'" This text has often been used as a theological justification for the persecution of Jews and for the charge that they are a deicide (God-killing) people.

Some scholars have even argued that there is so much anti-Jewish material in Matthew's Gospel that it could not have been written by a Jew. However, I (and most scholars today) am convinced that Matthew was a Jewish Christian and that he has written what is both a Jewish book and a Christian Gospel (to be treated in detail in chapters 8 and 9, respectively). I contend that the ways between Judaism and Christianity had not yet definitively parted, and that Matthew and his community viewed themselves as within Judaism and indeed fighting for its survival as best they knew how. The problem came in the second century onward, when the majority within the church were non-Jews who read the problematic passages in Matthew's Gospel through Gentile eyes—not as part of a family quarrel within Judaism but rather as reflecting a battle between two separate and hostile religions. While I do not consider Matthew's Gospel to be anti-Jewish in its origins and in itself, I do acknowledge its anti-Jewish potential when read apart from its original historical setting and with hostile intent. It is important that Christians today, especially preachers and teachers, be sensitive to this Gospel's anti-Jewish potential while appreciating what seems to have been the Evangelist's real aim: to place Jesus in his context of Judaism and to show how through Jesus the Jewish heritage may be preserved and made even more fruitful for all who call upon the name of the Lord God of Israel.

The six chapters that follow provide a narrative analysis of Matthew's Gospel. A narrative analysis attends to the characters and their interactions, the plot or structure of the story, the viewpoint of the narrator, and the times and places. Since this is a religious text, the analysis also considers the theological terms, concepts, and themes that are developed as the story unfolds.

There are, however, some other concerns that might contribute to a fruitful study of this particular Gospel:

- Keep in mind that Matthew's story has at least two levels— the time of Jesus' public ministry (A.D. 30), and the time of the Evangelist and his community (ca. A.D. 85).

- Since Matthew's Gospel is a revised and expanded version of Mark, look at the parallel passages in Mark (or Luke, for Q) and pay particular attention to what is unique or different in Matthew.

- Pay special attention to Matthew's uses of the Old Testament, and try to discern what authority it has in his theology.

- Try to understand why a Jewish reader today might take offense at Matthew's Gospel, and ask yourself whether this concern is justified.

- Having immersed yourself in the subtle literary expression and rich theology of Matthew's Gospel, ask yourself what special message it might have for the church and the world today.

• And reflect on how the wisdom of Jesus, preserved in the Sermon on the Mount and other parts of Matthew's Gospel, might affect how you look at your own experience and how you conduct yourself in everyday life.

For Reflection and Discussion

As you embark on this intellectual and spiritual journey, take stock of your own life and ask where you now stand. What is your goal in life, and how do you expect to get there?

What do you hope for from your serious engagement with Matthew's Gospel this year?

Do you think that anti-Judaism is a serious problem for Christians today? Why or why not?

PART TWO

Matthew's Story of Jesus

14

*In the time of King Herod, after Jesus was
born in Bethlehem of Judea, wise men from
the East came to Jerusalem, asking, "Where
is the child who has been born king of the
Jews? For we observed his star at its rising,
and have come to pay him homage." . . .
When they had heard the king, they set out;
and there, ahead of them, went the star that
they had seen at its rising, until it stopped
over the place where the child was. When
they saw that the star had stopped, they
were overwhelmed with joy. On entering
the house, they saw the child with Mary his
mother; and they knelt down and paid him
homage. Then, opening their treasure chests,
they offered him gifts of gold, frankincense,
and myrrh. And having been warned in a
dream not to return to Herod, they left for
their own country by another road.*

—Matthew 2:1–2, 9–12

2

Jesus' Origins and Beginnings
Matthew 1—4

Matthew's Gospel is a story about Jesus' birth, public ministry, and his passion, death, and resurrection. Even the larger sections of Jesus' teachings appear in the context of this overall story line. The Evangelist presents himself as a believer in Jesus' special importance and as the all-knowing narrator whose words can be trusted. He wrote originally for a largely Jewish-Christian audience that wanted greater clarity about how their faith in Jesus related to their identity as Jews in the late first century.

The main character is Jesus, and all the other characters relate to him whether positively (disciples), negatively (scribes and Pharisees), or neutrally (crowds). After the story of his birth, the plot follows the geographical-theological outline developed by Mark: Jesus' ministry in the Galilee area, his journey from Galilee to Jerusalem, his ministry in Jerusalem, and his passion and death there. All the action takes place in the land of Israel around A.D. 30.

This first large section in Matthew's Gospel concerns the circumstances surrounding Jesus' birth, his relationship to John the Baptist, and the beginnings of his public activity. The infancy narrative revolves around two questions: Who? (the identity of Jesus) and Where? (how the child Jesus who was born in Bethlehem came to grow up in Nazareth). Throughout the infancy narrative, Matthew emphasizes Jesus' roots in Judaism and how he fulfilled the Scriptures of Israel. He also foreshadows the events of the passion by his stress on confusion, conflict, and danger. The mood of Matthew's infancy narrative is much darker than Luke's consoling and even romantic version of the Christmas story.

The Genealogy and What It Means

With his genealogy, Matthew links Jesus with Israel's greatest king (David) and the founder of God's people (Abraham). With the three sections of fourteen ancestors each, he suggests that Jesus was born at the right or most "perfect" time ($7 \times 2 = 14$). By including several women who have dubious reputations, he prepares for the most unusual (virginal) conception of Jesus.

1:2–6a. The first section traces Jesus' ancestry from Abraham to David through Judah. These names were available from 1 Chronicles 1 and 2 and Ruth 4:18–22. The genealogy is presented in a linear pattern from one generation to another. The all-male list is interrupted by the appearance of three women: Tamar, who dressed as a prostitute and conceived children from her father-in-law, Judah (Genesis 38); Rahab, the prostitute of

Jericho, who aided Joshua and Caleb (Joshua 2); and Ruth the Gentile, who became the great-grandmother of David (Ruth).

1:6b–11. The section from David to the Exile first alludes to David's adulterous affair with Bathsheba (2 Samuel 11—12). It goes on to list the various kings of Judah. While Solomon, Hezekiah, and Josiah were among the best (though not without their own faults), the other kings, according to the judgment offered in 1 and 2 Kings, were generally not good.

1:12–17. Apart from the first three names, the section from the Exile to Jesus consists mainly of unknown figures. The break in the pattern near the end ("Joseph the husband of Mary, of whom Jesus was born") points forward to the account of Jesus' virginal conception that follows in 1:18–25. The genealogy ends with another mention of Abraham and David, and the counting of the three segments of fourteen generations.

Matthew's genealogy roots Jesus the Messiah in Israel's history as the people of God. By contrast, the genealogy of Jesus in Luke 3:23–38 traces his ancestry back through David and Abraham to Adam as the ancestor of all humankind. This is consistent with Luke's emphasis on Jesus as the "light for revelation to the Gentiles" (Luke 2:32). Matthew's genealogy provides a bridge between the Old and the New Testaments, and fits well with his emphasis on the Jewishness of Jesus.

Jesus' Birth and Early Years

1:18–25. In Matthew's account of Jesus' conception and birth, the major figure is Joseph. His willingness to go along with the divine plan revealed to him by an angel in a dream explains how Jesus the Son of God became the Son of David through Joseph as a descendant of David. While prepared for by the unusual women in the genealogy, the virginal conception and birth of Jesus go beyond even those unusual figures in the Messiah's genealogy. The child will be named Jesus, from the Hebrew *yashă*, "God saves," which points toward his adult role as savior of his people. His miraculous conception and birth are interpreted as the fulfillment of God's promise to King Ahaz in Isaiah 7:14: "the [virgin] shall conceive and bear a son." The name *Immanuel* ("God is with us") in the prophecy again points to Jesus' adult role as God's presence among us and to the promise from the risen Jesus at the end of the Gospel: "I am with you always" (28:20).

If the major question in Matthew 1 was "Who?" in chapter 2 it is "Where?" The various episodes explain how Jesus, who was born in Bethlehem, came to reside in Nazareth. Each of the five episodes features a place and contains a biblical quotation or allusion, suggesting that the new Messiah's itinerary proceeded according to God's will. In several respects the episodes recall the early chapters of the book of Exodus and serve to identify Jesus with Moses.

2:1–6. In the first episode, wise men from the east (the Magi) come to Jerusalem and inquire about the birthplace of the "king of the Jews"—that is, the Jewish Messiah. The Magi are Persian priests, but their observing the stars suggests some connection with Babylonian astronomy/astrology. Their arrival frightens Herod the Great, who ruled over Jerusalem and Palestine from 37 to 4 B.C. and whose own status as king of the Jews is tenuous both politically and religiously. The purpose of the Magi's visit is to do homage to Israel's Messiah. They learn from the chief priests and scribes summoned by Herod that the Messiah is to be born in Bethlehem of Judah according to Micah 5:1–2.

2:7–12. The second episode takes place in Bethlehem. The Magi follow the Scriptures and the star, and pay homage to the newborn child. The biblical text underlying the episode is the prophecy of Balaam in Numbers 24:17: "a star shall come out of Jacob, and a scepter shall rise out of Israel." Whereas Herod only pretends to want to do homage, the Gentile Magi do so with complete sincerity. The gifts they offer echo Isaiah 60:6 and Psalm 72:10. Their coming to the infant Jesus anticipates the command of the risen Jesus to "make disciples of all nations" (28:19). On the basis of a dream (a method of divine communication as in 1:20 and 2:13, 19), the Magi depart without informing Herod about the exact location of the child.

2:13–15. The third episode features Egypt, a place under Roman control but outside of Herod's dominion. Again Joseph acts in response to an angel's message delivered in a dream. The warning about Herod searching for the child in order to destroy him echoes Exodus 2:15 where Pharaoh seeks to kill Moses. Herod's death in 4 B.C. provides the occasion for the fulfillment of Hosea 11:1: "Out of Egypt I called my son." Note that the quotation suggests a close relationship between Jesus the Son of God and Israel as God's son in its exodus from Egypt.

2:16–18. The fourth episode, the slaughter of the male children under two years of age, takes place in and around Bethlehem. The biblical model is Pharaoh's decree to kill all the male Hebrew children in Exodus 1:15–22. The incident is said to fulfill the prophecy about Rachel weeping for her children in the vicinity of Bethlehem, according to Jeremiah 31:15.

2:19–23. The final episode explains why Jesus grew up in Nazareth of Galilee rather than in Bethlehem of Judea. Joseph is directed by an angel in a dream to return to the land of Israel because Herod is dead. The message in 2:20 ("those who were seeking the child's life are dead") again echoes Moses' story in Exodus 4:19. However, the political chaos in Jerusalem under Herod's son, Archelaus, between 4 B.C. and A.D. 6, makes Nazareth a safer place for the Messiah. The settling of the Messiah's family in Nazareth is again presented as fulfilling a biblical prophecy, "He will be called a Nazorean." The reference may be to Judges 13:5, 7 where a "nazirite" is someone especially devoted to God, or to Isaiah 11:1 where the Hebrew word for branch (*nezer*) refers to the Messiah.

The Adult Jesus and John the Baptist

3:1–6. Matthew's description of John the Baptist is a carefully edited version of Mark 1:2–6. Matthew presents John as preparing the way for Jesus and thus as subordinate to him. John's baptism involves moral conversion in preparation for the coming manifestation of God's kingdom. Matthew locates John's ministry in "the wilderness of Judea," the mountainous and desolate region east of Jerusalem. His summary of John's preaching in 3:2 is the same as his summary of Jesus' preaching in 4:17: "Repent, for the kingdom of heaven has come near." In quoting

Isaiah 40:3 he equates John with the "voice" and Jesus with "the Lord." Then he describes John's prophetic lifestyle modeled on that of Elijah (2 Kings 1:8), the popular enthusiasm that John evoked, and his rite of baptism in the Jordan River.

3:7–10. The context for the sample of John's teaching is the coming kingdom of God and the divine judgment that will accompany it. John urges sincere repentance because the time is short. His teachings here consist of three warnings: Do not imagine that merely undergoing the ritual of John's baptism will protect you, do not think that merely belonging to the children of Abraham (i.e., Israel) will save you, and do not waste the short time that is left. What John demands now is good deeds "worthy of repentance." This same teaching appears almost verbatim in Luke 3:7–9, and is generally assigned to the Sayings Source Q, the collection of Jesus' sayings used independently by Matthew and Luke. The most obvious difference is the audience: "the crowds" in Luke 3:7, and "many Pharisees and Sadducees" in Matthew 3:7. The latter group will be prominent among Jesus' opponents throughout Matthew's Gospel.

3:11–12. The second sample of John's teaching first contrasts the baptisms of John (with water) and Jesus (with "Holy Spirit and fire") and their persons—Jesus as the "one who is more powerful" and John as his servant. Then John uses the image of separating wheat (something good) from chaff (something bad or useless) to indicate what will happen at the divine judgment accompanying the full coming of God's kingdom.

3:13–17. When John baptizes Jesus in the Jordan River, a heavenly voice identifies Jesus as "my Son, the Beloved."

Unique to Matthew is the dialogue between John and Jesus about the propriety of this baptism, probably due to belief in Jesus' sinlessness (see Hebrews 4:15). Jesus' dismissal of John's objection ("to fulfill all righteousness") is most likely an appeal to God's will or plan. The three biblical symbols mentioned in 3:16–17a— the opening of the heavens, the descent of the Spirit of God, and the voice from heaven—all prepare the Jewish reader/listener for a divine communication. Then a heavenly voice identifies Jesus in biblical language: the Son of God (Psalm 2:7), the Beloved Son (Isaac, Genesis 22), and the Servant of God (Isaiah 42:1; 44:2).

Jesus' Temptation and the Beginning of His Ministry

4:1–11. What is generally called "the temptation of Jesus" is better entitled "the testing of God's Son." After the introduction, there are three dialogues between the "tempter" and Jesus, followed by a conclusion. Jesus' forty-day fast recalls the fasts undertaken by Moses (Deuteronomy 9:18) and Elijah (1 Kings 19:8). The close parallels with Luke 4:1–13 suggest that both Evangelists took the story from Q. The biblical background for the dialogues is Deuteronomy 6—8: Where ancient Israel failed in its testing in the wilderness, Jesus shows himself to be the faithful Son of God. The tests concern physical pleasure and satisfaction, spectacular display and fame, and political power. At each point Jesus refuses these temptations with a quotation from Deuteronomy (8:3; 6:16; and 6:13 respectively). Having seen what kind of Son of God Jesus is, the devil leaves him, and then the angels minister to him (see Mark 1:12–13).

The beginning of Jesus' public ministry takes place in Galilee. Matthew describes how Jesus came back to Galilee after his baptism and testing, how he called his first disciples by the Sea of Galilee, and how crowds came to Galilee to hear his teaching and to be healed by him.

4:12–17. Jesus made Capernaum, a small fishing village by the Sea of Galilee, the center of his activity in accord with the prophecy in Isaiah 9:1–2. The emphasis in Matthew's use of this biblical quotation is its reference to Galilee and Jesus' role as its light. But it also points to the risen Jesus' commission in 28:19 to make disciples of all the Gentiles.

4:18–22. Contrary to the usual Jewish practice, Jesus takes the initiative in choosing and summoning his first disciples from among Galilean fishermen (see Mark 1:16–20). The apparent lack of preparation, the simple and effective command ("follow me"), and the immediate and positive response indicate Jesus' natural charisma and attraction. The first followers are called to leave behind their families and businesses to fish for people (see Jeremiah 16:16).

4:23–25. Matthew summarizes Jesus' ministry of preaching and healing, describes the kinds of persons brought to him, and notes that crowds from Galilee and the surrounding areas converge upon Jesus. They, along with the disciples, will provide the audience for Jesus' Sermon on the Mount and his many miracles.

For Reflection and Discussion

What have you learned so far about who Jesus is?

Why is Matthew so insistent on showing that Jesus fulfilled Israel's Scriptures?

How does Jesus stand in relationship to John the Baptist?

3

Jesus Is Powerful in Word and Deed

Matthew 5—9

The first of Jesus' five major speeches in Matthew's Gospel is the Sermon on the Mount (5—7). It is followed by a collection of accounts about the miracles of Jesus (8—9). This section as a whole shows that Jesus is powerful in both word and deed.

Powerful in Word

Matthew used the Sermon on the Mount to gather Jesus' teachings from Q (see Luke 6:20–49), Mark, and his special source(s). The sermon consists of

- an introduction (5:1–20)
- six antitheses (5:21–48)
- three acts of piety (6:1–18)
- advice on various other topics (6:19—7:12)

"Do not think that I have come to abolish the law or the prophets; I have come not to abolish but to fulfill. For truly I tell you, until heaven and earth pass away, not one letter, not one stroke of a letter, will pass from the law until all is accomplished. Therefore, whoever breaks one of the least of these commandments, and teaches others to do the same, will be called least in the kingdom of heaven; but whoever does them and teaches them will be called great in the kingdom of heaven. For I tell you, unless your righteousness exceeds that of the scribes and Pharisees, you will never enter the kingdom of heaven."

—Matthew 5:17–20

- exhortations about putting these teachings into practice (7:13–27)
- a conclusion (7:28–29).

In its literary form the sermon is close to the wisdom instructions in the books of Proverbs and Sirach. It is concerned mainly with the character traits, values, and attitudes that should mark the followers of Jesus.

5:1–2. The audience for Jesus' first sermon is the crowd, along with the disciples (see 7:28–29). In the Bible, a mountain is often the place of divine revelation. The most obvious example is Mount Sinai (Exodus 19—24). By sitting down, Jesus assumes the posture of other Jewish teachers of his time.

5:3–12. The beatitudes declare as "happy" or "fortunate" persons who exhibit certain character traits or behaviors, and promise them rewards in the future fullness of God's kingdom. Matthew includes nine beatitudes in comparison with the four in Luke 6:20–23, which most likely represents the Q form. In two cases Matthew tends to spiritualize Jesus' points. For instance "blessed are the poor" becomes "blessed are the poor in spirit," and "blessed are those who hunger and thirst" becomes "blessed are those who hunger and thirst for righteousness." Most of the additional beatitudes in Matthew are rooted in biblical texts such as Isaiah 61 and Psalm 37.

5:13–16. Three images—the salt of the earth, the light of the world, and the city built on a hill—help define the identity and importance of those who follow Jesus faithfully. While rooted in Israel's identity as God's people (Isaiah 2:2–5), these images also allude to how significant are Jesus' followers to the well-being of the whole world.

5:17–20. In what is often regarded as the thesis statement of the Sermon on the Mount, Jesus insists that there is continuity between the Law and the prophets and his teachings ("not to abolish but to fulfill"). At the same time he presents himself as the authoritative interpreter of the Law, and challenges his followers to surpass the scribes and Pharisees in living according to God's will.

5:21–48. Jesus presents six antitheses. An antithesis sets one statement against another. However, Jesus' antitheses are more concerned with going to the roots of biblical commands than with contradicting them. In this way Jesus shows himself to be the authoritative interpreter of the Law rather than one who abolishes it. What he tells us essentially is, If you wish to avoid breaking the commandment against murder, avoid the anger that leads to murder. If you wish to avoid adultery, avoid lust. If you wish to avoid giving your wife a divorce document, avoid divorce entirely. If you wish to avoid false oaths or vows, avoid swearing at all. If you wish to avoid the law of retaliation, refuse to resist provocations to it. And if you wish to love your neighbor, love even those who seem to be your enemies and follow God's own example in doing so. Several of these antitheses contain additional sayings loosely related to the main topic.

6:1–18. Three important religious actions in the Judaism of Jesus' time were almsgiving, prayer, and fasting. Jesus challenges his hearers about how and why they should do these things. His principle stated in 6:1 is that if these acts of piety are really intended as worship of God, then they should be practiced without excessive display intended to impress other people. In each case—almsgiving, prayer, and fasting—Jesus contrasts how the hypocrites do it and what their reward is (a reputation for piety), and how "you" should do it and what your reward will be (from God).

The section on prayer also warns against verbosity in prayer, provides a sample prayer, and includes a warning about being willing to forgive others if you expect God to forgive you. The sample prayer is the Lord's Prayer in 6:9–13 (compare Luke 11:2–4). After a typically Jewish address stressing both the immanence ("Our Father") and the transcendence ("in heaven") of God, the prayer presents three "you" petitions about hallowing, or making holy, God's name, the coming of God's kingdom, and doing God's will. Then there are three "we" petitions for sustenance ("daily bread"), forgiveness, and protection in the time of testing. Taken as a whole, the Lord's Prayer primarily concerns the full coming of God's kingdom, which is Jesus' central theme in Matthew's Gospel.

6:19—7:12. This section is devoted to various other topics: treasures in heaven, a sound eye, serving two masters, avoiding needless worry, judging others, profaning the holy, persistence in prayer, and the "golden rule"—"do to others as you would have them do to you." The variety of topics and the apparent lack of logical progression are typical of Jewish (and other ancient Near Eastern) wisdom instructions.

7:13–27. The concluding exhortations insist that Jesus' teachings are to be lived out in everyday life. The emphasis on practice is also typical of Jewish wisdom instructions. The images of the gate and the way, the tree and its fruits, saying and doing, and building houses on rock or sand all stress the need to put into practice Jesus' teachings in this sermon and elsewhere.

Each of the great speeches in Matthew's Gospel concludes in the same way: "when Jesus had finished saying these things." Matthew also reminds us that "the crowds" were included among the audience and were duly impressed by the personal authority with which Jesus taught.

Powerful in Deed

To show that Jesus is powerful not only in word but also in deed, Matthew gathers miracle stories from Mark and Q into three cycles, interrupted by teachings about discipleship. As a careful editor, Matthew omits what he regarded as unnecessary details. The effect is to highlight the encounters with Jesus and to turn the miracle stories into examples of praying faith.

8:1–4. After making the transition from the sermon to the miracles, Matthew rewrites Mark 1:40–45. He streamlines the story by omitting references to Jesus' emotions; he has the leper address Jesus as "Lord" and focuses on the dialogue between Jesus and the leper. Like in Mark's Gospel, Jesus demonstrates respect for the laws pertaining to leprosy in Leviticus 13—14.

8:5–13. The story of the healing of the centurion's servant (see also Luke 7:1–10) is told in order to emphasize the power of Jesus' word. The Gentile military man knows the power of verbal commands and so trusts that Jesus can heal his servant even without physical contact. Matthew uses this example of faith as an opportunity to include Jesus' saying about Gentiles coming to enjoy the heavenly banquet with Israel's patriarchs in 8:11–12 (see Luke 13:28–29). Unlike Luke's account, in which Jewish intermediaries approach Jesus on the centurion's behalf (see Luke 7:1–10), in Matthew he enters directly into a dialogue of faith with Jesus.

8:14–17. Matthew shortens Mark's account about the healing of Peter's mother-in-law and his summary of Jesus' many other healings (see Mark 1:29–31). The result is a sharper focus on Jesus and the power of his word. By adding the quotations of Isaiah 53:4 ("He has borne our infirmities and carried our diseases"), Matthew suggests that by his healings Jesus fulfills Israel's Scriptures and proves himself to be the suffering servant who takes upon himself the misery of others.

8:18–27. In rewriting the episode of the stilling of the storm in Mark 4:35–41, Matthew has Jesus take the initiative in going over to the eastern shore of the Sea of Galilee. He interrupts the story with challenging sayings from Q (see Luke 9:57–60) about discipleship: Do not expect a stable and comfortable existence, and look on discipleship as overriding even the most solemn human obligations such as burying one's parents. Then Matthew places Jesus in the lead and the disciples "following" him into the boat. When the great storm arises and the boat is being swamped, the disciples awaken Jesus and cry out in the language of prayer, "Lord, save us! We are perishing!" In response Jesus scolds them for their "little faith"—Matthew's typical term for the disciples' imperfect response to Jesus. Then Jesus stills the storm, something that in the Old Testament only God can do (see Psalm 107:23–30). The disciples' question—"What sort of man is this?"—is an implicit recognition of Jesus' divinity.

8:28–34. Matthew's version of the healing of the Gadarene demoniacs is considerably shorter and less graphic than the sprawling account of the Gerasene demoniac in Mark 5:1–20. The effect of Matthew's edit highlights the demoniacs' questions in 8:29 (see Mark 1:21–25): "What have you to do with us, Son of God? Have you come here to torment us before the time?"

9:1–8. Likewise, Matthew's compression of the account of the healing of the paralyzed man in Mark 2:1–12 underscores the point that Jesus is powerful in deed (healing) and in word (by declaring the man's sins forgiven).

9:9–17. Based on Mark 2:13–22, the interlude between the second and third cycles of miracle stories contains more teachings about discipleship. It begins with Jesus calling Matthew the tax collector to "follow me," then explains who can become disciples of Jesus (even tax collectors and sinners) and what actions are appropriate to them (not necessarily those performed only by conventionally religious persons). Matthew's version is distinctive for naming the tax collector as Matthew (see 10:3), for Jesus quoting Hosea 6:6 ("I desire mercy, not sacrifice," see 12:7), and for the final comment ("both [old and new] are preserved").

9:18–26. Jesus heals the centurion's daughter and the woman with the flow of blood. Matthew shortens the account found in Mark 5:21–43, which puts the emphasis on the petitioners' requests and Jesus' responses in word and deed. Thus he manifests his power over disease and death in response to their expressions of faith.

9:27–31. Matthew joins the healings of two blind men in Mark 8:22–26 and 10:46–52. Once more, leaving out some of Mark's details turns the episode into a prayer dialogue that emphasizes Jesus' healing power.

9:32–34. The healing of the mute demoniac (see Mark 7:31–37) leads to a split between the onlookers. Neither group denies the fact of Jesus' power. What they debate is the *source* of Jesus' power. Is it from God or from "the ruler of the demons?"

9:35–37. After repeating the summary of Jesus' activities used previously in 4:23, Matthew prepares for the list of the twelve apostles and the missionary discourse in chapter 10. The need for this missionary activity is expressed with the biblical images of the flock ("sheep without a shepherd") and the harvest (a plentiful harvest but few laborers).

For Reflection and Discussion

In light of the Sermon on the Mount, how might you describe the ideal follower of Jesus?

How does the Sermon on the Mount shape and guide your life? How would you like it to shape and guide your life?

How and why does Matthew emphasize the power of Jesus' word and the theme of prayerful faith in the miracle stories?

*He left that place and entered their syna-
gogue; a man was there with a withered
hand, and they asked him, "Is it lawful to
cure on the sabbath?" so that they might
accuse him. He said to them, "Suppose one
of you has only one sheep and it falls into a
pit on the sabbath; will you not lay hold of it
and lift it out? How much more valuable is a
human being than a sheep! So it is lawful to
do good on the sabbath." Then he said to the
man, "Stretch out your hand." He stretched
it out, and it was restored, as sound as
the other. But the Pharisees went out and
conspired against him, how to destroy him.*

—Matthew 12:9–14

4

Jesus' Mission: Acceptance and Rejection
Matthew 10—12

In his second major discourse, Jesus commissions his apostles to share in his mission of proclaiming God's kingdom and healing those most in need. Nevertheless, he receives at best a mixed reception. While no one denies Jesus' extraordinary powers, his opponents (especially the scribes and Pharisees) raise questions about the source of his powers. Are they from God or from Satan? Jesus vigorously defends the divine origin of his mission, and invites those with eyes to see to learn from him as the wisest teacher of all and to become part of his true family made up of those dedicated to doing the will of God.

10:1–4. Jesus gathers his twelve disciples and commissions them to do what he has been doing in chapters 8 and 9: performing exorcisms and healings. The number twelve evokes the image of the twelve tribes of ancient Israel and suggests that the disciples' mission is to participate in Jesus' program for the restoration of Israel. The twelve apostles are listed in six pairs. Other slightly different lists appear in Mark 3:16–19; Luke 6:14–16; and Acts of the Apostles 1:13. Matthew specifies Simon (Peter) as first, since he was among the first disciples called by Jesus and serves as the spokesman for the group throughout Matthew's Gospel. He also identifies Matthew as a tax collector and presumably the same person mentioned in 9:9. Whether the second Simon in 10:4 was a Canaanite, a Zealot, or simply religiously zealous, is not clear. The description of Judas as the one who betrayed Jesus points to his actions in the events leading to Jesus' crucifixion.

10:5–15. In commissioning the twelve apostles, Jesus tells them where to go, what to do, how to live, and how to respond to rejection. They are to avoid Gentile and Samaritan territories; the mission to all nations will come after Jesus' resurrection (28:16–20). Rather, now they are to focus their energies on "the lost sheep of the house of Israel" (see 9:36). They are to do what Jesus has been doing so far in Matthew's story: proclaiming God's kingdom (3:2; 4:17) and healing those in need. In the service of their mission they are to live as simply as possible, avoid excess baggage, and rely on the hospitality of others for their food and lodging. When and if such hospitality is not forthcoming, they are to move on and carry out their mission elsewhere, leaving any thought of vengeance to God's final judgment. For Sodom and Gomorrah as symbols of lack of hospitality, see Genesis 19 and Ezekiel 16:49.

10:16–25. In the second part, Jesus forecasts the suffering the disciples will face as they carry out their mission, and he explains suffering as a consequence of following him. After an opening statement, Jesus describes two dangerous situations and offers two promises of help and a concluding reassurance. The danger to the disciples (like sheep among wolves) demands from them both shrewdness and innocence. The dangerous situations involve public persecutions and divisions within families. In the first case Jesus promises help from the Holy Spirit, while in the second case he promises vindication at the coming of the Son of Man. The basic principle is this: As the teacher/master (Jesus) goes, so the disciples/slaves will go. Just as Jesus suffers persecution and conflict, so his disciples must expect the same.

10:26–42. The final part consists of various sayings about fear, acknowledging Jesus, family divisions, and acceptance by others. The exhortations about not giving in to fear are based on trust that at the Last Judgment all will become clear and that God has special care for the followers of Jesus. In the divine judgment the pivotal criterion will be whether someone has publicly acknowledged or denied Jesus. Then Jesus returns to the topic of divisions over him within families, suggesting that belonging to his new family overrides other family obligations, and challenges his followers to take up the cross and so find real life and genuine freedom. The final section gives further theological depth to the missionary discourse by proposing that those who accept Jesus' disciples ("these little ones," see 25:40, 45) accept Jesus himself and in turn accept his heavenly Father who has sent him.

11:1. The customary ending of Jesus' speech ("when Jesus had finished") provides a transition from his teaching back to the story (though there is a large amount of teaching even here), and from Jesus instructing his disciples to his public

activity of teaching and proclaiming the kingdom of heaven.
We do not hear anything about the disciples' return from their
missions or their successes or failures, as we do in Luke's account
(Luke 10:17–20).

The next segment consists of three units taken from Q that
consider the relationship between John the Baptist and Jesus.

**11:2–6. The first unit (see Luke 7:18–23) deals with John's
inquiry about Jesus, "Are you the one who is to come?"** John
sends word from prison (see 4:12; 14:1–12), and wants to know
whether Jesus is doing the work of the Messiah, and therefore
whether Jesus really is the Messiah. Jesus' response correlates
closely with the descriptions of his miracles in Matthew 8—9
and with Isaiah 35:5–6. Those who were expecting a military
and/or political Messiah would have been disappointed in Jesus'
reply. Such persons would have taken offense or been scandalized
by Jesus the teacher and healer.

**11:7–15. The second unit (see Luke 7:24–28) treats Jesus'
assessment of John the Baptist.** John exercised his ministry in
the Judean Desert near the Jordan River and by his lifestyle identified himself with the prophet Elijah (see 3:4). Those who went out
to see John would not have found a weak and shifting person ("a
reed shaken by the wind") or someone dressed like a royal courtier
("in soft robes"). In Matthew's Gospel these images point to the
account of John's death under Herod Antipas (14:1–12). Rather
they would have found not only a prophet of God's kingdom but
even an Elijah figure who was preparing the way for the day of
the Lord and for the Messiah (Malachi 4:5–6), thus fulfilling the
prophecy in Malachi 3:1. Despite John's greatness as "more than a

prophet," a new age has begun through Jesus, though in the face of great opposition that began with the earlier prophets and John. The bottom line is that John was an Elijah figure who prepared for Jesus' ministry and the day of the Lord.

11:16–19. The third unit (see Luke 7:31–35) is a parable about the negative responses to both John and Jesus among their contemporaries. The children in the marketplace comment critically on the failure of their playmates to respond to either their happy games (weddings) or sad games (funerals). When faced with John's ascetic lifestyle, people said, "He has a demon." When faced with Jesus' celebratory lifestyle, they made personal attacks on him as a glutton and a drunkard. Jesus says simply that "wisdom is vindicated by her deeds," that is, "you will know them by their fruits" (7:20).

11:20–24. Jesus criticizes three cities in Galilee—Chorazin, Bethsaida, and Capernaum—for failing to respond correctly (by repenting) to the miracles that Jesus performed in them or their vicinity. Tyre and Sidon, which were cities on the Mediterranean coast in southern Lebanon, had been the object of prophetic threats in the Old Testament (see Isaiah 23:1–12; Ezekiel 28:11–23). In Genesis 19 Sodom is destroyed because of its inhospitality and moral perversity. Jesus' point is that if his miracles had been performed even in those notorious places, the people would have repented. Since the Galilean cities have not responded properly to him, they will fare even worse at the coming judgment.

11:25–30. In the midst of material devoted largely to opposition and conflict, Jesus' declaration stands out as

a bright light. He praises God for having revealed the content and significance of his teaching to lowly and insignificant persons. His address, "Father, Lord of heaven and earth," neatly summarizes the biblical understanding of God as close to us (immanent) and above us (transcendent). Jesus also identifies himself as the pivotal mediator of divine revelation, as the one who reveals God's wisdom to humankind. Then Jesus the wisdom teacher promises "rest" to those who carry heavy burdens, and he describes himself as "gentle and humble in heart." What Jesus says about himself, his school, and his teaching is remarkably similar to what Jesus Ben Sira, a wisdom teacher in Jerusalem in the early second century B.C., says about himself and his school in Sirach 51:23–30.

The two controversies that follow—about plucking grain and healing on the Sabbath—present Jesus as the authoritative teacher whose burden is light in comparison with that of the Pharisees.

12:1–8. When the disciples pluck grain to eat (see Mark 2:23–28), they are doing what was allowed by the law in Deuteronomy 23:25. What the Pharisees object to is their doing it on the Sabbath, because it seems like work (more specifically, reaping). In response to their objection, Jesus first appeals to the example of David in 1 Samuel 21:1–6 when he allowed his men to eat the bread of the presence (Leviticus 24:5–9), and then to the fact that even priests in the Jerusalem temple have to do work on the Sabbath in order to offer their sacrifices. The "something greater" in 12:6 seems to be Jesus himself (the Son of David), the kingdom of God, and the community he is shaping. Jesus goes on to quote Hosea 6:6 again ("I desire mercy and not sacrifice," see 9:13) and to proclaim himself as "lord of the Sabbath."

12:9–14. The second Sabbath episode takes place in "their synagogue," where the opponents are again Pharisees (see Mark 3:1–6). The man's withered hand is presumably a chronic condition, perhaps a birth defect. The Pharisees' complaint is that Jesus could have waited until after the Sabbath to perform the healing. In his defense Jesus puts forward the case of rescuing a sheep that has fallen into a pit on the Sabbath. In contrast to the more rigorous Essenes (the group behind the Dead Sea scrolls), Jesus here sides with the Pharisees in allowing the animal to be rescued. How much more then should they allow Jesus to heal a human person on the Sabbath! The healing that takes place then is immediate and complete. Nevertheless, the Pharisees are not only not convinced by Jesus but even conspire to have him killed.

12:15–21. Instead of mounting active resistance against the Pharisees and their conspiracy, Jesus departs, takes up his healing ministry again, and urges silence about himself and his deeds. Matthew has greatly abbreviated Mark 3:7–12 and added a quotation from Isaiah 42:1–4, which is from the first of the "Servant" songs in Isaiah. The main point of the quotation here seems to be its reference to the Servant's meekness and gentleness. He does "not wrangle or cry aloud." The passage also identifies Jesus as the Servant, the one beloved by God (see Matthew 3:17 and 17:5), the bearer of the Holy Spirit, and the source of hope for the Gentiles (see Matthew 28:16–20).

12:22–37. Jesus' healing of a possessed man who is blind and mute evokes different responses from the crowds ("Can this be the Son of David?") and from the Pharisees ("It is only by Beelzebul, the ruler of the demons"). In response to them, Jesus first shows that Satan could not be the source of his healing power since his exorcisms are blows against Satan's kingdom. Jesus' saying about his exorcisms being proof that in Jesus' ministry "the kingdom of God has come upon you" indicates that his miracles are present manifestations of God's reign and pointers toward its full coming. Then Jesus observes that attributing his power to Satan is the unforgivable sin of blasphemy against the Holy Spirit, and that his good deeds place him on God's side while his opponents (the Pharisees) appear to be on Satan's side.

12:38–42. Despite Jesus' many miracles and defenses, the scribes and Pharisees want further authentication of his ministry. In response Jesus offers only "the sign of the prophet Jonah," which in Matthew is Jesus' death and resurrection (12:40; see Jonah 1:17; 2:10). Whereas the Queen of Sheba came a long distance to hear Solomon's wisdom (1 Kings 10:1–13), the scribes and Pharisees reject Jesus' even greater wisdom in their own land.

12:43–50. The parable about the evil spirit returning suggests that the exorcisms performed by Jesus may offer only a temporary respite from the power of Satan, and that an even worse period is in store for "this evil generation." However, it is possible to find refuge and genuine kinship in the true family of Jesus, that is, among those who do "the will of My Father in heaven."

For Reflection and Discussion

How might you apply to your own life the values underlying Jesus' missionary discourse in Matthew 10?

Why do you think Jesus aroused such resistance and opposition from his contemporaries? How do you think people would respond to him today?

What might the passages about the wisdom school of Jesus (11:25–30) and the new family of Jesus (12:46–50) contribute to your understanding of the church?

Then Jesus told his disciples, "If any want to become my followers, let them deny themselves and take up their cross and follow me. For those who want to save their life will lose it, and those who lose their life for my sake will find it. For what will it profit them if they gain the whole world but forfeit their life? Or what will they give in return for their life?"

—Matthew 16:24–26

5

The Kingdom of God and the Suffering Messiah

Matthew 13—17

Jesus' third lengthy teaching clarifies aspects of God's kingdom through a series of analogies or parables. However, despite his wise teachings and marvelous actions, he meets misunderstanding and hostility from various sources, including his own disciples. As he and his disciples begin their journey up to Jerusalem, he tries to get them (and us) to confront the fact that he is a *suffering* Messiah.

13:1–3a. Jesus sits in a boat while teaching the crowds on the shore. Matthew takes this scene from Mark 4:1–2. The presumed audience for most of the first part of Jesus' third great discourse in 13:1–35 is the "crowds." Jesus speaks to them mainly in parables. At 13:36 the audience shifts to the disciples.

A parable is a story taken from nature or everyday life. It features something strange or unusual, which in turn stimulates the audience to think about some even more important reality in fresh ways. Jesus used parables to talk about the kingdom of

God, to explain what God's kingdom is and will be like, and how one can become part of it. Comparison with familiar earthly realities was an appropriate way of teaching about what in its fullness is a transcendent and future reality. In chapter 13, Matthew drew heavily upon Mark 4:1–34 and expanded it with material from Q and his special source(s). His major concern was with the acceptance and rejection of Jesus' preaching of God's kingdom. That is, why did some understand and act on Jesus' preaching, while others did not?

13:3b–9. The first parable features a sower who scatters his seeds in four different locations. The parable is introduced by a summons to pay attention ("Listen!") and concludes with another such summons ("Let anyone with ears listen!"). The story develops a threefold pattern and leads to a reversal at the end. There is nothing wrong with the sower or the seed. Indeed, we are supposed to equate the sower with Jesus and the seed with his message about God's kingdom. The problem is with the soils in which the sower sows the seed. The first three kinds of soils—the path, the rocky ground, and the thorns—fail to yield anything useful. By contrast, the good soil brings forth a spectacularly large harvest. The message to the crowds (and to Jesus' disciples) is that even though some reject Jesus' preaching, those who accept it will more than make up for those who do not.

13:10–17. The interlude between the parable and its interpretation provides sayings that develop the theme of accepting and rejecting Jesus and his message. When the disciples inquire why Jesus speaks to the crowds in parables, Jesus distinguishes between them as insiders and the crowds as outsiders, and he states that he reveals to the disciples the secrets of the kingdom of heaven. Next Jesus paraphrases and then quotes Isaiah 6:9–10, thus suggesting that the mixed reception by the crowds is what a prophet can expect, and that such a response is in accord with God's will expressed in Scripture. Jesus declares his disciples to be "blessed," even more blessed than the prophets and righteous persons of old, for having the privilege to see and hear Jesus.

13:18–23. The interpretation of the parable identifies further the reasons why some reject and some accept Jesus' message, and it describes the different kinds of soils: superficial understanding, persecution, and the cares of the world and the lure of wealth. By contrast the good soil represents those who hear the word and understand it, and thus bear huge amounts of fruit (good works). Some of the vocabulary in the interpretation sounds more like what appears in the New Testament epistles rather than in the Gospels. Many scholars suggest that this interpretation arose within the early church and reflects the experiences of some who initially accepted the gospel but fell away for various reasons, and of those who accepted it and did great things with it.

The remaining parables in Matthew 13 are introduced by the phrase "the kingdom of heaven is like . . ."

13:24–30. As with the parable of the sower, the parable of the wheat and the weeds deals with the mixed reception of Jesus' preaching about God's kingdom. The harvest is a familiar biblical image for divine judgment (see Jeremiah 51:33; Hosea 6:11; Joel 3:13). The parable counsels patience and tolerance in the present, and encourages leaving the task of separating good and evil persons to God at the Last Judgment. For Jesus' detailed interpretation of this parable for the disciples, see 13:36–43.

13:31–33. The twin parables of the mustard seed and the yeast contrast the kingdom's small beginnings in Jesus' preaching with what will be the great results when it arrives in its fullness. They also suggest that the kingdom's development is going on in the present.

13:34–43. The parables thus far have been directed to the crowds (but see 13:10–17, where Jesus gives an explanation to the disciples). The explanation of the parable of the weeds and the wheat (and what follows) is supposedly for the benefit of the disciples. The explanation first makes seven identifications: the sower is the Son of Man, the field is the world, the good seed is the children of God's kingdom, the weeds are the children of the evil one, the enemy is the devil, the harvest is the end of this age, and the reapers are angels. Then in 13:40–43 there is a short apocalypse in which the Son of Man will have the angels gather and destroy all the wicked and will make the righteous shine like the sun.

13:44–46. A second pair of parables about buried treasure and the precious pearl emphasizes the extraordinarily great value of God's kingdom. It is in fact so valuable that a person should respond to it with total commitment and enthusiasm.

13:47–50. The parable of the fishing net comes with an interpretation. Matthew presents it much as he did the earlier parable of the wheat and the weeds. The fish caught in the net need to be separated between good (edible and kosher) and bad. Likewise, at the Last Judgment God will have angels separate evil persons from the righteous and will mete out their appropriate punishments and rewards.

13:51–53. What the disciples should have understood is that God's kingdom has small beginnings, receives a mixed reception, is moving toward a future fullness, and will bring with it a divine judgment. The ideal scribe (like the Evangelist) brings together what is new (what God has done in and through Jesus) and what is old (the heritage of Israel as God's people). This third discourse ends in the usual way ("When Jesus had finished . . .").

13:54–58. Jesus is rejected at the synagogue in Nazareth. Matthew takes his account from Mark 6:1–6. The townspeople's basic question—"Where did this man get this wisdom and these deeds of power?"—concerns the origin of Jesus' power as a teacher and healer. Matthew edits Mark's account by specifying the place as "their" synagogue, identifying Jesus as "the carpenter's son" (not "the carpenter"), and noting that Jesus "did not do many" (instead of "could do no") deeds of power there." Throughout the centuries the brothers and sisters of Jesus have been variously identified as his full siblings, stepsiblings, or close relatives such as cousins. The second and third explanations are in keeping with the doctrine of Mary's perpetual virginity.

14:1–12. In recounting the death of John the Baptist, Matthew abbreviates and simplifies Mark 6:14–29. The result is to highlight the contrast between John the fearless prophet and Herod Antipas the vain and foolish political leader. Herod's guess that Jesus might be John brought back to life leads by flashback to how Herod had executed John. The law that Herod broke was

Leviticus 18:16. Herod's foolish promise ("whatever she might ask") leads him to have John beheaded and his head served on a platter. John's fate points to Jesus' death.

14:13–21. The feeding of the five thousand appears in all four Gospels (see Mark 6:35–44; Luke 9:12–17; John 6:1–15). Matthew's juxtaposition of Herod's grisly and squalid banquet and Jesus' compassionate and caring banquet is striking. At Herod's royal banquet there is pride and arrogance, scheming and murder. At Jesus' banquet in the wilderness, there is healing, trust, and sharing. The biblical model for Jesus' banquet is the prophet Elisha's feeding of a hundred men with twenty barley loaves (see 2 Kings 4:42–44). The way in which Jesus' banquet is described points to the Last Supper (26:26–29) and the messianic banquet in the kingdom of God. Matthew heightens the miraculous element by noting that besides the five thousand men, the "women and children" were also fed.

14:22–36. In his account of Jesus walking on water, Matthew follows Mark 6:45–56. After making the disciples take him back to the western shore of the Sea of Galilee, Jesus spends time in prayer and then meets them on the sea where they are struggling against a strong wind (see 8:23–27). In stilling the storm Jesus does what only God can do according to Psalm 107:29, and in walking on water Jesus does what only God can do according to Job 9:8. In identifying himself ("It is I"), he uses a formula that God uses of himself in Isaiah 41:4 and 43:10. Thus the event is a revelation or epiphany of Jesus' divine nature.

Matthew's most distinctive addition comes in 14:28–31, where Peter tries to do what Jesus is doing. While successful at first, Peter soon loses courage and begins to drown. So he prays to Jesus, "Lord, save me!" The disciples correctly recognize Jesus as "the Son of God" and worship him. When they land on the western shore, Jesus heals many sick people. Touching the fringe of Jesus' garment happened before when he healed the woman with the flow of blood (9:20–21).

15:1–20. The debate about the tradition of the elders concerns customs and rules surrounding the Old Testament Law, not the Law itself (compare Mark 7:1–23). Jesus' opponents are Pharisees and scribes, who take special interest in such customs and rules. They inquire why Jesus' disciples do not wash their hands before eating. The issue here is not hygiene but ritual purity. Jesus dismisses the matter as mere custom and gives another example of their confusing human traditions and divine commands. He accuses them of encouraging others to declare their property or money "sacred" and dedicated to God (*qorban*) to avoid fulfilling the biblical command to honor one's parents by supporting them in their old age. Citing Isaiah 29:13, he contends that the Pharisees and scribes are so intent on promoting their human traditions that they ignore divine commands. In 15:10–14 the audience is the crowd. Here Jesus declares that moral (internal) purity is more important than ritual (external) purity. He also characterizes the Pharisees as "blind guides." Then in response to Peter's request, Jesus reiterates the difference between moral purity and ritual purity, and illustrates moral impurity with a list of vices. Throughout, Matthew is careful not to push Jesus' teachings as far as Mark did with his comment that Jesus "declared all foods clean" (Mark 7:19).

15:21–28. In rewriting Mark 7:24–30, Matthew emphasizes this woman's identity as non-Jewish by calling her a "Canaanite" and turns the Markan story into more of a dialogue of praying faith. When the woman calls on Jesus as "Lord, Son of David," Jesus claims that he "was sent only to the lost sheep of the house of Israel" (see 9:36; 10:6). When she prays again ("Lord, help me"), he responds again that that his mission is to Jews ("the children") and not to Gentiles ("dogs"). However, the Canaanite women finally gets the better of Jesus when she notes that even the dogs get fed from the crumbs of the master's table. Jesus marvels at her faith and rewards it by healing her daughter. This is the only case in the Gospels where Jesus seems to lose a debate—and to a Gentile woman!

15:29–31. Matthew transforms the healing of the deaf man with a speech impediment in Mark 7:31–37 into a general healing session for persons with various infirmities. Several of these afflictions are mentioned in Isaiah 35:5–6, and so Jesus fulfills that prophecy.

15:32–39. As in Mark 8:1–10, Matthew presents a second multiplication of loaves and fishes. Some interpreters find in the number seven (seven loaves, seven baskets of leftovers) a reference to Gentiles (the seventy nations of the world). Matthew emphasizes the disciples' role as intermediaries between Jesus and the crowd, continues the Eucharistic dimension, and expands the crowd of four thousand by adding "women and children."

16:1–12. This passage involves two incidents concerning Pharisees and Sadducees (see Mark 8:11–21). First they join forces to trap Jesus into trying to perform some spectacular sign, and fail at it. Rather than falling into their trap, Jesus criticizes them for failing to read the signs happening during Jesus' ministry that point toward the presence of God's kingdom. Here, the sign of Jonah probably refers to the repentance of tax collectors and sinners (as in Luke 11:30, but not Matthew 12:40). Then, when conversing with his disciples, Jesus warns them against the "yeast" (most likely, corrupt teaching) of the Pharisees and Sadducees. When they think he is talking about actual bread, Jesus reminds them of the two multiplications of loaves and makes clear that he is referring to the teaching of the Pharisees and Sadducees. In Matthew's Gospel, Jesus' characterization of his disciples as having "little faith" is a much milder rebuke than what they receive in Mark 8:14–21.

16:13–20. At Caesarea Philippi (in northern Galilee) Jesus asks his disciples about who people say that he is (see Mark 8:27–30). To Mark's list Matthew adds Jeremiah, whose sufferings as a prophet in Jerusalem prefigured those of Jesus. Matthew also extends Peter's confession of Jesus as the Messiah to include "the Son of the living God." Then Matthew inserts Jesus' blessing of and promise to Peter. Jesus first declares Peter "blessed" because he has received a divine revelation concerning Jesus' identity. Then he promises to build his church (see 18:17) upon Peter as its rock (a play on his name) and to defend it against the powers of sin and death. Finally he gives Peter the power to admit people to God's kingdom (see Isaiah 22:15–25) and to make authoritative decisions on earth (see 18:18). His order that the disciples not tell anyone he is the Messiah leads into his prediction of his suffering and death, which illumines what kind of Messiah Jesus is.

16:21–27. In the first of three passion predictions (see 17:22–23 and 20:17–19), Jesus describes in detail what awaits him in Jerusalem. When Peter refuses to accept Jesus as a suffering Messiah, Jesus rebukes him as a tempter ("Satan") and reduces Peter the "rock" to a "stumbling block." Then he reminds his disciples (see 10:38–39) that those who follow him must be ready to suffer as he will. The picture of the Son of Man as judging everyone according to his or her deeds points to the judgment scene in 25:31–46. And Jesus' mention of those disciples who will not die before they see the Son of Man's coming leads into the transfiguration.

17:1–13. The transfiguration of Jesus (see Mark 9:2–13) provides the inner circle of his followers—Peter, James, and John—with a preview of the glory that will belong to Jesus after his resurrection. The event takes place on a mountain (a favorite setting for divine revelations). In the presence of Moses and Elijah, who represent the Law and the Prophets, a voice from the heavens identifies Jesus as God's Son and Servant in the same words used at Jesus' baptism in 3:17. Though Peter wishes to prolong the experience, Jesus prefers to move forward to Jerusalem and the cross, and he interprets the experience as a vision (17:9). The idea that Elijah must return before the Day of the Lord is based on Malachi 3:23–24 (or, in some Bible translations, 4:5–6). Matthew very clearly identifies John the Baptist with the prophet Elijah, and Jesus links his sufferings to those of John (see 14:1–12).

17:14–20. Jesus heals a possessed boy. Matthew abbreviates the long and colorful account of this in Mark 9:14–29 and shifts the focus from the father's faith to the disciples' little faith. In approaching Jesus, the father adopts a posture of prayer (kneeling), says "Lord, have mercy on my son," and so exhibits again Matthew's theme of praying faith. Jesus in turn cures the boy instantly and attributes the disciples' failure to their "little faith" (6:30; 8:26; 14:31; 16:8). Their little faith contrasts with the perfect faith shown by Jesus himself. For the mustard seed as a symbol of God's kingdom, see 13:31–32. For God's ability to move mountains, see Isaiah 40:4; 49:11; and 54:10.

17:22–23. Jesus makes his second prediction about his betrayal, execution, and resurrection (see Mark 9:30–32). Whereas in Mark, the disciples are confused but afraid to say anything, Matthew notes that they are saddened by Jesus' predictions.

17:24–27. The temple tax was levied on Jews to help support the upkeep of the Jerusalem temple (see Exodus 30:11–16; Nehemiah 10:32). The logic of this peculiar episode is that since the temple is the house of God and Jesus is the Son of God, he and his followers have no obligation to pay that tax. However, lest other Jews regard their failure to pay the tax as a renunciation of Judaism, the necessary coin is miraculously supplied in the mouth of a fish and so Jesus' dignity as the Son of God is not compromised.

For Reflection and Discussion

In light of Jesus' parables in Matthew 13, how would you describe the kingdom of heaven?

Why did so many people misunderstand and reject Jesus? What were they expecting from a messiah? What did Jesus say and do that confused or put them off?

How do you react to the idea of a suffering Messiah? Why do you suppose suffering had to be part of Jesus' identity?

6

Jesus' Way to Jerusalem
Matthew 18—23

As Matthew's Jesus continues his journey to Jerusalem, he offers advice about problems among his followers and addresses such topics as marriage and divorce, riches as an obstacle to discipleship, and greatness in God's kingdom. Then when he arrives in Jerusalem, he takes symbolic action in the temple, enters into debates with various opponents, offers more parables about God's kingdom, and denounces the scribes and Pharisees as hypocrites.

The fourth major speech in Matthew's Gospel has been described as advice to a divided community. The first part deals with status seeking, scandal, and apostasy. The second concerns reconciliation to the community and willingness to forgive.

18:1–5. Matthew smoothes over the unseemly dispute among Jesus' disciples as told in Mark 9:33–34 and turns it into a simple question about greatness in God's kingdom. Jesus responds by acting out a parable; he places a child in their midst. In Jesus' world children had no political significance or social status. He then interprets his action by recommending

58

"Jerusalem, Jerusalem, the city that kills the prophets and stones those who are sent to it! How often have I desired to gather your children together as a hen gathers her brood under her wings, and you were not willing! See, your house is left to you, desolate. For I tell you, you will not see me again until you say, 'Blessed is the one who comes in the name of the Lord.'"

—Matthew 23:37–39

---

humility as the necessary qualification for greatness in God's kingdom. Only those who recognize their own insignificance before God can be truly great. This is what the Bible means by "fear of the Lord." Those who welcome such persons welcome Christ himself (see 10:40–42 and 25:31–46).

18:6–14. The topic now shifts from children to "little ones" (simple believers) and the serious sin involved in being a stumbling block (*skandalon*) to them. While recognizing that scandals may happen, Jesus insists that everything possible must be done to prevent those who perpetrate scandals from repeating them. Then he warns against despising the "little ones" and notes that each of them has a guardian angel. Matthew's version of the good shepherd parable in 18:12–14 (see Luke 15:4–7) indicates the special care that should be taken to seek out those little ones who may have gone astray in order that they not be totally lost.

The major teaching on community that takes up the rest of chapter 18 revolves around the themes of reconciliation and forgiveness.

18:15–20. Jesus outlines a three-step process for reconciling an offender to the community: a one-on-one encounter, a small-group intervention, and a hearing before the whole community. Then he bestows on the community the power to bind and loose, as he did on Peter in 16:19. Finally he promises to be present in the process by which the community arrives at its decisions.

18:21–35. How many times can a straying member be forgiven and reconciled? Jesus answers Peter's question first by giving a number (either 77 or 490 times, depending on the manuscript reading) so large that it suggests unlimited forgiveness. Then in the parable of the unforgiving servant, he illustrates in a dramatic way the petition of the Lord's Prayer according to which God's willingness to forgive us demands that we also be willing to forgive others who may have offended us (6:12, 14–15). Those who have experienced God's mercy must show mercy to others. Otherwise, they can expect to experience the full effect of God's justice.

19:1–2. Jesus now moves from Galilee to Judea. By going by way of Perea across the Jordan, he avoids going through Samaria. He attracts large crowds, principally because of his healing powers.

19:3–9. Matthew rewrites Mark's version (10:2–12) of Jesus' debate with the Pharisees about marriage and divorce. By adding "for any cause," he shifts the debate from the legality of divorce to grounds for divorce. Then he rearranges the biblical material. By quoting Genesis 1:27 and 2:24 first, he stresses that divorce was not part of God's original intent. Then he refers to the permission for divorce in Deuteronomy 24:1–4 and attributes it to Moses' recognition of the people's hardheartedness. Finally he quotes Jesus' absolute prohibition of divorce (see also Mark 10:11–12; Luke 16:18; 1 Corinthians 7:10–11) but inserts an exception for "unchastity" (*porneia*) as in 5:32 (see also 1 Corinthians 7:15). The term *porneia* may refer to sexual misconduct or to marriage within forbidden degrees of kinship.

19:10–12. In this passage, which is unique to Matthew, the disciples wonder at the strictness of Jesus' teaching and suggest that it may be better not to marry at all. In rejecting their suggestion, Jesus recommends celibacy but only if it is taken up voluntarily "for the sake of the kingdom of heaven."

19:13–15. By laying hands on little children (see Mark 10:13–16), Jesus calls down God's blessing upon them and transmits his own holiness to them. In the face of his disciples' objections, Jesus insists that the children be allowed to come to him and holds them up as good examples of receiving the kingdom of heaven as a gift from God since small children necessarily receive everything as gifts (see 18:1–4).

The three passages in 19:16–30 follow Mark 10:17–31, with some important variations.

19:16–22. In Jesus' encounter with the rich young man, Matthew smoothes out the dialogue and inserts the commandment about loving one's neighbor (Leviticus 19:18). By including the phrase "if you wish to be perfect," Matthew seems to leave room for two grades of religious observance: keeping the commandments, and following Jesus as a disciple. Even though the rich young man declines Jesus' invitation to follow him as a disciple, it appears that by keeping the commandments he can still "enter into life."

19:23–26. In Jesus' instruction about the dangers of wealth, Matthew follows Mark 10:23–27 closely, apart from omitting the disciples' puzzlement at Jesus' teaching. Whereas wealth was often viewed as a sign of God's blessing, Jesus suggests that it can more often be an obstacle to entering God's kingdom.

19:27–30. In Jesus' promise of rewards for following him (see Mark 10:28–30), Matthew inserts a picture of "the

renewal of all things" when the Twelve will join the Son of Man in glory and judge the twelve tribes of Israel. He also omits Mark's mention of persecutions. The saying about the great reversal in 19:30 appears again in 20:16, at the end of the parable of the workers who are paid in reverse order of their being hired.

20:1–16. The parable of the workers in the vineyard consists of two parts: the hiring of the workers and their payment. It must be read against the background of the vineyard as a symbol for Israel (see Isaiah 5:1–7) and the harvest as a symbol for the Last Judgment. In the first part the landowner goes to the marketplace and hires day laborers to harvest in his vineyards at several different times. The accounting takes place at the end of the day, in the vineyard. What is surprising is that the owner instructs his manager to pay the last ones hired first and to pay everyone the same amount. When the first ones hired grumble, the owner explains his practice as just and fair (since they had agreed on the payment), and defends it as a case of his desire to be generous. The parable thus defends Jesus' ministry to tax collectors and sinners, and explains why the spiritual latecomers will receive the same reward (the kingdom of heaven) as the scribes and Pharisees. The reversal saying in 20:16 (see 19:30) applies to the order of payment, and not to the reward (which is the same for all).

20:17–28. Matthew follows the pattern in Mark 10:32–45: passion prediction, misunderstanding, and correction. This third passion prediction is more detailed than the first two (16:21 and 17:22–23). Whereas in Mark, James and John misunderstand, Matthew blames their mother, thus softening Mark's image of the Twelve (but showing an insensitivity to women).

Jesus refuses her request for places of special prominence at the banquet in God's kingdom. Instead, he promises a cup of suffering that he and his disciples will have to share. In doing this, Jesus articulates his ideal of leadership as the service of others. His greatest service will be giving his life as a "ransom" for many and thus rescuing them from the power of sin and death.

20:29–34. The healing of the two blind men is clearly based on the story of Bartimaeus in Mark 10:46–52, which Matthew already used in 9:27–31. Matthew portrays their healing as an example of the healing power and compassion of Jesus as the Son of David. He also heightens the element of dialogue and thus develops further the theme of praying faith ("Lord, let our eyes be opened").

21:1–11. Matthew's account of Jesus' entrance into Jerusalem (see Mark 11:1–10) highlights the fulfillment of Scripture. Jesus makes his entry from the Mount of Olives, where according to Zechariah 14:4 a great end-times battle will take place. Jesus enters the city as the humble Messiah. The bizarre picture of him seated on two animals—a donkey and a colt—reflects an excessively literal reading of Zechariah 9:9. The use of palm branches evokes rituals connected with the Jewish festivals of Tabernacles and Hanukkah. The crowd greets Jesus with the words of Psalm 118:26 and identifies him as the prophet from Nazareth.

21:12–17. Jesus goes directly into the temple area and performs a symbolic action in upsetting the commercial operations of those who changed currency and sold doves in connection with the sacrifices being offered there (see Mark

11:11, 15–19). Jesus justifies his actions on the grounds of Isaiah 56:7 and Jeremiah 7:11. Matthew mentions Jesus healing the blind and the lame, the kind of persons prohibited from entering the temple complex according to 2 Samuel 5:8. When the chief priests and scribes try to prevent the children from hailing Jesus as the Son of David, Jesus defends them on the basis of Psalm 8:2. Then Jesus goes to Bethany, a small village east of Jerusalem.

21:18–22. The episode of the fig tree (see Mark 11:12–14, 20–25) is unusual since Jesus seems to act irrationally and out of anger. The biblical background is Jeremiah 8:13: "When I wanted to gather them, says the Lord, there are no grapes on the vine, nor figs on the fig tree" (see also Hosea 9:10, 16). Jesus' action is symbolic of the opposition he will find in Jerusalem and points to its eventual destruction in A.D. 70. From this incident Jesus draws lessons about the power of prayer.

Jesus' return to the temple area sets off a series of controversies or debates, which is interrupted by three parables. This material highlights the opposition to Jesus on various fronts and his own wisdom and cleverness.

21:23–27. The first controversy (see Mark 11:27–33) concerns the source of Jesus' authority. Here the opponents are the chief priests and elders. Rather than answering their question directly, Jesus asks them their opinion about the source of John the Baptist's authority. Not only does Jesus elude their trap, but he also puts them on the defensive and reduces them to saying, "We do not know."

21:28–32. Jesus uses the parable of the two sons to defend his own (and John's) ministry to tax collectors and sinners,

and to criticize his opponents for failing to do God's will and recognize Jesus as God's prophet. The first son (i.e., tax collectors and sinners) initially refuses the father's request to work in the vineyard but eventually complies. The second son (i.e., chief priests and elders) agrees to go but never does any work. Which son did the father's (God's) will?

21:33–46. The parable of the vineyard (see Mark 12:1–12) builds on the vineyard as a symbol for Israel in Isaiah 5:1–7. The landowner (God) makes all the preparations and leases his vineyard to tenant farmers (i.e., the religious and political leaders of Israel). At harvest time he sends slaves (i.e., prophets) to collect the produce but they are abused by the tenants. Finally he sends his son (Jesus) on the grounds that they will respect him. However, the tenants kill the son in the hope of obtaining the vineyard for themselves. When the father learns of his son's fate, he will destroy the tenants (Israel's leaders in A.D. 70) and give the vineyard to others (Jesus' followers). The imminent death and resurrection of the Son is taken to fulfill Psalm 118:22–23 in which Jesus as the rejected stone becomes the cornerstone. Note that the vineyard is not destroyed (as it is in Isaiah 5:1–7). There is, however, a change in leadership in the vineyard. The chief priests and Pharisees recognize that they are the tenant farmers and that the parable is about them.

22:1–14. The third parable in the series, the royal wedding banquet (see Luke 14:15–21), concerns those who reject and those who accept Jesus' invitation to God's kingdom. The audience is the same as that for the preceding parable, the chief priests and Pharisees. Likewise, the "slaves" sent to issue the invitation are the prophets, who are not only rejected but also abused and killed. The excuses offered by those first invited are trivial. The king's response is rage at their insolence. The description of his reaction in 22:7 points to what happened in Jerusalem in A.D. 70. The second round of invitations is issued indiscriminately to anyone who will come, good and bad alike. The point of what may have once been an independent parable, the man without a wedding garment, is that it is not enough to "enter" God's kingdom. Rather, those who enter must behave appropriately once they are inside.

22:15–22. The series of controversies is resumed (see Mark 12:13–17) with the debate about paying taxes to the Roman emperor. The opponents are Pharisees (members of a Jewish religious movement) and Herodians (supporters of the Herod dynasty). Working together, they hope to trap Jesus. If Jesus agrees with the Herodians that it is lawful to pay taxes to the emperor, he will lose prestige with the insurgents against Roman occupation. If he disagrees and sides with the Pharisees, the Roman officials and their Jewish supporters may have him arrested and punished. But Jesus eludes their trap by demonstrating that both groups use Roman coins and so are already in the Roman system. He goes on to challenge them to be as observant about fulfilling their obligations to God as they are in paying taxes to Caesar.

22:23–33. The opponents in the controversy about resurrection (see Mark 12:18–27) are Sadducees, a Jewish movement that rejects belief in resurrection. In this matter, Jesus sides with the Pharisees, who are strong proponents of resurrection. The case proposed by the Sadducees concerns a woman who marries seven brothers in turn, after each one dies (see Deuteronomy 25:5–10). Whose wife will she be in the resurrection? Jesus responds by noting that these Sadducees "know neither the scriptures nor the power of God." He claims that resurrected life is more like angelic life, and so does not involve marriage. Moreover, he contends that the references to the God of Abraham, Isaac, and Jacob in the Torah (Exodus 3:6, 15–16) imply that those patriarchs are still alive, and that he is the God of the living. Thus belief in resurrection really is present in the Torah.

22:34–40. In the debate about the greatest commandment (see Mark 12:28–34), the opponents are Pharisees. Their question was also put to other famous Jewish teachers of the time, such as Hillel and Shammai. Jesus responds by naming two commandments: love of God (Deuteronomy 6:4–5), and love of neighbor (Leviticus 19:18). The image of the whole Law and Prophets hanging from these two commandments suggests that they provide the key to carrying out all the other 611 commandments in the Torah.

22:41–46. The opponents in the final debate (Mark 12:35–37) are again Pharisees. When Jesus asks them whose son the Messiah is, they answer, "David's" (see Isaiah 11:1, 10; Jeremiah 23:5). Jesus responds by quoting Psalm 110:1 ("the Lord said to my Lord"). The traditional author of the psalm was David himself. But David has Yahweh ("the Lord") speaking to the Messiah ("my Lord"). Since David refers to the second figure as "my Lord," the Messiah is not merely David's son but rather is God's Son. Thus Jesus again outwits his opponents and silences them.

In chapter 23 Matthew takes Mark's brief denunciation of the scribes (12:38–40) and turns it into a major attack against the scribes and Pharisees. Whereas in the controversies in the preceding chapters Jesus was often on the defensive, now he takes the offensive. The audience here is the crowds and his disciples.

23:1–12. While acknowledging the authority of the scribes and Pharisees, Jesus criticizes them on multiple fronts. They do not practice what they preach; they burden others with their traditions while not acting upon them themselves; they cultivate a false reputation for holiness through ostentatious religious and public displays; and they insist on honorific titles (Rabbi, Father, Instructor). By contrast Jesus' followers have only one teacher (Jesus), and embrace his ideals of leadership as the service of others and humility rather than self-promotion.

23:13–31. The seven woes against the scribes and Pharisees are Matthew's adaptation and expansion of Q material found in Luke 11:37–52. The basic charge against them is hypocrisy—that is, the gap between saying and doing, and between appearance and reality. The Matthean Jesus accuses them of the following:

1. preventing access to God's kingdom,
2. making converts to their movement who turn out to be worse than they are,
3. engaging in foolish, hair-splitting arguments regarding oaths and vows,
4. being more concerned with small issues in the Law than with its major concerns,

5. pursuing external matters at the expense of internal matters,

6. insisting more on ritual purity than on moral integrity,

7. and building monuments to dead prophets while rejecting and plotting against prophets in their own time such as John and Jesus.

23:32–39. In the final warning (see Luke 11:49–51; 13:34–35), Jesus first suggests that scribes and Pharisees might as well fill up the quota of wickedness before the Last Judgment and accept their sentence to hell. Then he indicts them for mistreating the prophets, sages, and scribes sent to God's people. Finally he offers a lament over Jerusalem and prophesies the destruction of its temple as just punishment for abusing and murdering the emissaries God sent there.

For Reflection and Discussion

What problems, if any, treated in Matthew 18 and 23 are similar to those facing the church today?

What do the various parables in Matthew 20—22 contribute to your understanding of the kingdom of God?

What character traits stand out in Matthew's Jesus as he makes his way to Jerusalem and exercises his ministry there?

7

Jesus' Final Discourse, and His Death and Resurrection

Matthew 24—28

Jesus' final speech in Matthew 24—25 is often called his eschatological discourse because it deals mainly with the end of human history as we know it (*eschaton* means "last") and the coming of God's kingdom in its fullness. In the first half (24:1–36) Matthew follows Mark 13:1–32 closely, though he does rearrange, adapt, and add some material. In the second half (24:37—25:46) he includes parables from Q and his special source(s) to encourage further attitudes of faithful service of God in the present and continuing vigilance with regard to the future. This last speech leads into the story of Jesus' suffering, death, and resurrection in chapters 26—28.

24:1–14. The beginning of Jesus' eschatological discourse follows Mark 13:1–8, while the second part (24:9–14) is an adaptation of Mark 13:9–13 (which Matthew had used already in 10:17–25). Taking up his prophecy of the temple's destruction in 23:38, Jesus predicts that "not one stone will be

While they were eating, Jesus took a loaf of bread, and after blessing it he broke it, gave it to the disciples, and said, "Take, eat; this is my body." Then he took a cup, and after giving thanks he gave it to them, saying, "Drink from it, all of you; for this is my blood of the covenant, which is poured out for many for the forgiveness of sins. I tell you, I will never again drink of this fruit of the vine until that day when I drink it new with you in my Father's kingdom"

—Matthew 26:26–29

left here upon another." While seated on the Mount of Olives
(see Zechariah 14:4), he is asked by his disciples about the signs
of his second coming and the end of the present age. He begins
by dampening their expectations. Before these things can happen, there will occur the appearance of false messiahs, wars and
rumors of wars, and famines and earthquakes. In characterizing
these events as "the beginning of the birth pangs," he evokes the
Jewish concept of the Messiah's coming as accompanied by suffering and testing. He further extends the timetable by forecast-
ing persecutions against his followers, apostasies and betrayals by
some, and spiritual apathy. He promises that those who endure
patiently will be saved and contends that the good news of God's
kingdom must first be preached to the Gentiles before the end
can come.

**24:15–31. The description of the "great tribulation" and
the coming of the Son of Man (Mark 13:14–23) is heavily
dependent on the book of Daniel for its language and imag-
ery.** The "desolating sacrilege" traditionally translated as "the
abomination of desolation" originally referred to the desecration
of the Jerusalem temple under the Syrian king Antiochus IV
Epiphanes in 167 B.C. (see Daniel 9:27; 11:31; 12:11). Here it refers
to some event in the first century A.D. or further into the future.
The event will come suddenly and inflict terror and suffering on
many. The admonition in 24:20 to pray that it not happen on
the Sabbath suggests that the members of Matthew's community
were still strict Sabbath observers. The hope is that God might
shorten the time period for the sake of his chosen ones (24:22).
As in 24:5, there is a warning against false messiahs and prophets

who might lead the people astray. The coming of the Son of Man will be preceded by cosmic portents; the list of them consists of phrases taken from various parts of the Old Testament. His coming is described in 24:30 in the language of Daniel 7:13–14. It will signal the time for the Last Judgment and the vindication of the elect ones.

24:32–36. When will all this happen? On the one hand, these sayings suggest that it will take place very soon ("in this generation"). However, no one except the Father—neither the angels nor the Son—knows the exact time. Therefore one should always be prepared and act as if the Day of the Lord were to come in the very next moment.

24:37–51. This series of short parables promotes faithfulness and constant watchfulness. Jesus speaks of Noah and the flood, the two men in the field, the two women grinding meal, the thief in the night, and the two servants. While the Son of Man's coming is certain, it will happen suddenly and without much warning. So always be on guard!

25:1–13. The long parable of the ten bridesmaids reinforces the points made in the short parables. The scene is the bridegroom bringing his new bride to his house or that of his father, after making all the legal arrangements with the father of the bride. The ten bridesmaids were supposed to escort the wedding party as it drew close to home. However, the wedding party was delayed. Five bridesmaids brought along a good supply of oil for their lamps, but another five did not. While the foolish ones were off buying more oil, the wedding party arrived. When the foolish bridesmaids finally make it back to the bridegroom's house, the door has been shut and they are denied admittance. The moral of the story regarding the coming of God's kingdom is, "Keep awake therefore, for you know neither the day nor the hour."

25:14–30. The parable of the talents (large sums of money) insists on the importance of wise and decisive action in the present. A man going on a journey entrusts five, two, and one talent, respectively, to three servants. On his return, he holds an accounting. The first two servants doubled his money, and so he praises them, entrusts them with more, and admits them to his household. But the third servant who was given only one talent buried it and made nothing more with it. So the master is angry with him, dismisses him as worthless, and throws him out of his household. The moral of this story is, Make the best of the present, and God will reward you at the Last Judgment.

25:31–46. This end-times discourse reaches its climax with this scene of the Last Judgment. The Son of Man is the judge, and those to be judged are "all the nations." He will separate them into two groups—as a shepherd separates sheep and goats. The Son of Man commends those on his right hand for their acts of compassion to him when they fed him, gave him drink, welcomed him, clothed him, cared for him when he was sick, and visited him in prison. Asked when they did all these things, the Son of Man reveals that in doing these actions to "the least" they were doing them to him. Then he condemns those at his left hand for failing to perform these actions. Asked when they failed to do so, the Son of Man answers that in not doing them for "the least," they neglected to do them to him. The result of this Last Judgment scene is that "these will go away to eternal punishment, but the righteous into eternal life."

In Matthew's account of Jesus' passion, he follows Mark 14—15 closely while making some deletions and additions along the way. In what follows, the emphasis will be on Matthew's distinctive contributions.

26:1–16. Matthew follows Mark 14:1–11 in developing a contrast between the betrayal and scheming of Judas and the Jewish leaders on the one hand and the generosity of Jesus and the unnamed woman on the other. The plotters conspire to have Jesus killed quickly and quietly, and they pay Judas thirty pieces of silver, which is the compensation paid for a slave who has been killed (Exodus 21:32). The woman, however, is remarkably generous in anointing Jesus with expensive ointment, and she plays a prophetic role in identifying Jesus as the Messiah (the Anointed One) and preparing him for burial. Matthew omits some details about the perfume and has the disciples object to the woman's wastefulness.

26:17–29. Both Matthew and Mark (14:12–25) understand Jesus' Last Supper as a Passover meal. In his somewhat abbreviated account of the preparations, Matthew emphasizes Jesus' foreknowledge: "My time is near." In Jesus' prophecy that one of his disciples would betray him, Matthew has Judas say explicitly, "Surely not I, Rabbi?" In describing the institution of the Lord's Supper, Matthew follows what had probably already become part of a liturgical ritual and turns Mark's description of Jesus' action with the cup into a direct statement ("Drink from it . . ."). He also notes that Jesus' blood will be shed "for the forgiveness of sins."

26:30–35. After the meal, on the Mount of Olives (see Mark 14:26–31), Jesus prophesies his disciples' desertion of him as fulfilling Zechariah 13:7: "I will strike the shepherd, and the sheep of the flock will be scattered." His promise to meet them in Galilee after his resurrection points forward to his appearance there in 28:16–20. His correction of Peter's boast that he would never deny Jesus anticipates the account of his threefold denial in 26:69–75.

The arrest of Jesus takes place in the garden of Gethsemane ("the oil press") on the Mount of Olives. Matthew locates two episodes there: Jesus' prayer and the disciples' weakness and the capture of Jesus.

26:36–46. In the first episode (see Mark 14:32–42), Matthew heightens the role of Jesus. He directs his disciples' movements, prays three times with the same words, and recognizes that his hour has come. Matthew also softens Mark's emotional description of Jesus and makes the disciples seem less weak. At the end Jesus faces his fate and even embraces it as his Father's will.

26:47–56. In the second episode (see Mark 14:43–52), which describes Jesus' arrest, Matthew heightens the guilt of Judas by providing an interchange with Jesus ("Rabbi . . . Friend"). He also uses the incident of one of Jesus' disciples cutting off the ear of the high priest's slave as the occasion for Jesus to explain that he is letting all this happen to him so that the

Scriptures might be fulfilled. Matthew also omits the strange episode of the young man fleeing naked in Mark 14:51–52. Taken
as a whole, the episode makes even clearer than Mark does that
Jesus willingly went to his death on the cross because he perceived it to be his Father's will expressed in the Scriptures and not
because he was a political revolutionary.

**26:57–75. In the account of Jesus' trial before the Jewish
council, Matthew follows Mark 14:53–72 even to the point
of preserving the "sandwich" structure that contrasts the
weakness of Peter (26:57–58, 69–75) and the fidelity of Jesus
(26:59–68).** The false witnesses claim that Jesus said he could
destroy the temple and build it in three days, while the high
priest accuses Jesus of blasphemy. At what appears to be the low
point in Jesus' life (his condemnation by the leaders of his own
people), only then does he accept and embrace the three great
titles of Messiah, Son of God, and Son of Man. Matthew makes
explicit, or clarifies, some details in Mark's account: Peter came
to the high priest's house "to see how this would end"; the officials sought false witnesses; Jesus could have destroyed the temple; the officials mocked Jesus; Peter's denials involved oaths; and
Peter's speech pattern identified him as a Galilean.

In his account of Jesus' trial before the Roman governor
Pontius Pilate, Matthew clarifies some points in Mark 15:1–20.
He also makes additions about Judas's suicide, the dream of
Pilate's wife, and Pilate's washing his hands of Jesus' condemna-
tion and the crowd's taking responsibility for it.

**27:1–10. Matthew explains why the chief priests and
elders met in the morning ("in order to bring about his**

death") and why they handed Jesus over to Pilate. Matthew's account of Judas's suicide (see Acts 1:18–19) stresses Judas's violent death on recognizing that he had betrayed "innocent blood" (Deuteronomy 27:25) and that the chief priests' use of the thirty pieces of silver to buy the potter's field ("the Field of Blood") fulfilled Zechariah 11:13. In other words, these events took place according to God's will as revealed in the Scriptures.

27:11–14. In Pilate's questioning of Jesus (see Mark 15:2–5), Matthew identifies him as the "governor" three times, and includes the elders among Jesus' accusers. The expression "King of the Jews" was Pilate's Gentile (mocking) translation of "Messiah." Jesus' silence before him fulfills Isaiah 42:2 and 53:7, and Pilate's amazement fulfills Isaiah 52:15.

27:15–26. Matthew emphasizes the choice that the people had to make between Jesus of Nazareth and Jesus Barabbas. He adds the report about the dream of Pilate's wife that affirms the innocence of Jesus just as Pilate is coming to his decision. He also adds Pilate's symbolic action in washing his hands of the matter (see Deuteronomy 21:6–9; Psalm 26:6) and his explicit declaration of Jesus' innocence, as well as the crowd assembled before him taking responsibility for Jesus' death "on us and on our children." For Matthew this latter addition most likely referred to those in Jerusalem in A.D. 30 who sought Jesus' death ("on us") and those in A.D. 70 who were among the victims of the Roman destruction of Jerusalem in A.D. 70 ("on our children"). Despite his recognition of Jesus' innocence, Pilate nevertheless releases Jesus Barabbas the revolutionary and hands Jesus of Nazareth (the Messiah) over to be crucified.

27:27–31. Matthew's account of the soldiers' mockery of Jesus is more orderly than Mark 15:16–20. The soldiers put a scarlet robe (one of their own, and not royal purple) and a crown of thorns on Jesus, thus playing off the image of the Roman emperor. Then they kneel before Jesus, acclaim him ("Hail, King of the Jews"), spit on him, and strike him on the head. The irony that trumps their irony is that Jesus really is the King of the Jews and superior even to the Roman emperor.

27:32–44. The irony continues in the account of the crucifixion. Crucifixion was applied to slaves and rebels, and its public character was intended to deter other potential insurgents. This explains the charge "King of the Jews," which Pilate meant ironically as if to say that this is what happens to those who pretend to be the Jewish Messiah. However, the double irony is that Jesus really is the Messiah and thus the King of the Jews. Taking his cue from allusions to Psalm 22 and Isaiah 53 in Mark 15:21–32, Matthew adds to them from Psalm 69, thus reinforcing the theme that everything is proceeding according to the Scriptures. The bystanders' mockery in 27:40 ("If you are the Son of God") echoes Satan's temptations in 4:3 and 4:6. The mockers repeat the two charges from the trial before the Jewish council: Jesus promised to destroy the temple, and claimed that he was the Son of God.

27:45–54. Matthew's account of Jesus' death (see Mark 15:33–39) is full of biblical allusions and symbolic events. For darkness at noon, see Amos 8:9 and Exodus 10:22. For Jesus' last words, see Psalm 22:1, which are the first words in the lament of the righteous sufferer. It is important to read the whole of Psalm 22, which emphasizes also the sufferer's trust in

God and his ultimate vindication. The bystanders misunderstand Jesus' words as a call for help from Elijah. The death of Jesus is told in 27:50 with remarkable restraint ("then Jesus . . . breathed his last"), perhaps with a reference to his sending forth the Holy Spirit. At the moment of Jesus' death, the curtain of the temple is torn in two, thus signifying a new phase in the history of salvation. In 27:51b–53 (only in Matthew) there are cosmic signs and resurrections of the dead, thus fulfilling Ezekiel 37:11–14. Finally even the centurion overseeing Jesus' execution has to confess, "Truly this man was God's Son!"

27:55–66. In describing the burial of Jesus (see Mark 15:40–47), Matthew lists the women who witnessed Jesus' death. The most prominent is Mary Magdalene. She saw Jesus die, witnessed his burial, found his tomb empty on Easter Sunday, encountered the risen Jesus, and informed the male disciples. Joseph of Arimathea gained possession of Jesus' corpse and allowed it to be interred in his new burial complex outside the walls of Jerusalem. Thus he fulfilled the biblical commandment to bury someone who had been hanged or crucified before evening (see Deuteronomy 21:22–23). Matthew identifies Joseph as a disciple of Jesus and omits Mark's note that he was a member of the Jewish council (which had condemned Jesus). Among the four Gospels, only Matthew, in 27:62–66, mentions the guard placed at Jesus' tomb as a precaution against claims that Jesus had been raised from the dead. See 28:4 and 28:11–15 for their ineffectiveness and how it came to be explained.

28:1–10. Matthew follows the empty tomb story in Mark 16:1–8, but clarifies some details and gives it a very different

ending in 28:8b–10. He first makes it clear that the same women who witnessed Jesus' death and burial came to Jesus' tomb on Easter Sunday morning. Next he notes that a great earthquake accompanied the opening of the tomb, despite the guard's presence. Then he identifies Mark's "young man" as an angel of the Lord. Next he claims that the guards fainted out of fear. Then the angel interprets the emptiness of the tomb as due to Jesus' resurrection and points to his appearance in Galilee. But rather than being reduced to silence and afraid to tell anyone (as indicated in Mark's version), the women according to Matthew become joyful and want to inform the male disciples about what they saw. Along the way they encounter the risen Jesus, embrace him (thus emphasizing his bodily resurrection), and worship him. Finally Jesus himself points to his appearance in Galilee.

28:11–15. Unique to Matthew is the report about the guards. Having fainted out of fear (28:4), they recount what happened to the chief priests, who in turn conspire with the elders to bribe the guards to keep them from telling what really happened. And so they put out the story that Jesus' disciples stole his body.

28:16–20. Matthew's final appearance account in Galilee is the climax of the whole Gospel. It takes place on an unnamed mountain (see 5:1–2; 17:1–8). The witnesses are the eleven disciples (minus Judas). While they all worship him (see 2:1–12), apparently some still doubt that he has really been raised from the dead. To the eleven (and to the church throughout "the age") Jesus issues what has come to be known as "the great commission" in 28:18b–20. After assuring them that all authority has been given to him (see Daniel 7:14), he tells them to make disciples of "all nations" (see 2:1–12), to baptize them, and to teach what he himself has taught. And he promises to be with them (see 1:23) until the full coming of God's kingdom ("to the end of the age").

For Reflection and Discussion

How might Matthew's emphasis on fidelity and watchfulness in light of the uncertain timing of the Son of Man's coming affect your Christian life? Does it encourage or frighten you?

Why is Matthew so intent on showing that Jesus' death and resurrection took place according to the Scriptures?

What does the risen Jesus' appearance in Galilee (28:16–20) reveal about the gospel, or good news? How might it challenge you and the church today?

PART THREE

Distinctive Features
of Matthew's Gospel

"Or have you not read in the law that on the sabbath the priests in the temple break the sabbath and yet are guiltless? I tell you, something greater than the temple is here. But if you had known what this means, 'I desire mercy and not sacrifice,' you would not have condemned the guiltless. For the Son of Man is lord of the sabbath."

—Matthew 12:5–8

8

A Jewish Book

Matthew's Gospel is the most Jewish of the four Gospels. From the beginning of Jesus' genealogy with Abraham to the risen Jesus' promise to be with his disciples always and thus fulfill the prophecy of "Emmanuel" (28:20; see 1:23 and Isaiah 7:14), Matthew calls upon traditional Jewish figures and concepts to bring out the true significance of Jesus. He expects his readers to know and respect the Jewish Scriptures, to be sensitive to Jewish modes of argument and debate, and to appreciate positively his portrayal of Jesus as a faithful Jew in a Jewish setting.

Yet for all his learning and literary artistry, Matthew seems also to have written during one of the most painful and chaotic periods in Jewish history, during which the Jerusalem temple was destroyed, creating a crisis both religious and political. Jews no longer had the temple as their religious center, and they had even less political autonomy in Palestine than they had before the Jewish Revolt of A.D. 66–73. These events posed a new set of questions: Where is Israel now? Who carries on the biblical traditions? Who is the heir to the biblical promises? Matthew wrote in such an environment, and these questions appear to have been on his mind.

This chapter will deal first with Matthew's concrete historical setting in the crisis that confronted all Jews, especially those in the eastern Mediterranean world, as a result of the Roman capture of Jerusalem and the destruction to the temple in A.D. 70. Then it will consider Matthew's distinctive treatment of some issues that were controversial among Jews of his time (Sabbath observance, purity rules, and divorce) and his arguments against his Jewish opponents. (In this and in the following chapter I have revised and adapted material from a pair of articles first published in 1993 in *Priests & People*, a British Catholic magazine now entitled *Pastoral Review*.)

Jews in an Unsettled Time

Matthew wrote good Greek. There is no surviving evidence proving that he wrote his Gospel first in Hebrew or Aramaic. Since Matthew wrote for a largely Jewish-Christian community in a city where there was a substantial Jewish population, his audience must have been Greek readers and Greek speakers. The atmosphere is that of the eastern Mediterranean world, not that of Italy or Greece or Asia Minor (present-day Turkey). There is a Semitic flavor to his language and thought. The most commonly assigned location of this writing is Antioch in Syria, though one can make a case for Caesarea Maritima and Damascus. Several passages (21:41; 22:7; 27:25) suggest a date of composition fifteen or twenty years after the Roman capture of Jerusalem and the temple's destruction.

Within Judaism of the late first century were other responses to the crisis of the temple's destruction and the breakup of Jewish nationalism. Two large apocalypses—*4 Ezra* (i.e., 2 Esdras 3–14) and *2 Baruch*—dealt with the present evil fortunes of Zion. While related to the destruction of the First Temple in 587 B.C., both books were clearly speaking about the Second Temple and trying to explain why it had been destroyed and how God's promises to Israel could ever be fulfilled. Their solution is apocalyptic or eschatological: Rome's rule is temporary; the intervention of God's Messiah will bring about Rome's defeat and the vindication of Israel; and the final outcome will involve resurrection, judgment, rewards and punishments, and the kingdom of God on earth. Both works seem to have expected this intervention and vindication to occur soon. In the meantime the faithful within Israel should prepare themselves by careful observance of the Mosaic Law as the revelation of God's will for the present. With the loss of the land and the destruction of the temple, only the Law remained among the three great pillars of historic Israel.

Another and more lasting Jewish response to the events of A.D. 70 was the early rabbinic movement or "formative Judaism." Although the earliest rabbinic writings come from around A.D. 200, the movement that produced them began to take shape after A.D. 70 at Yavneh (on the Mediterranean coast) under the leadership of Rabban Yohanan ben Zakkai. This movement involved several currents within first-century

Judaism: priestly traditions, legal debates, the scribes, and the Pharisees. The priestly strand contributed a lively interest in ritual purity, and the scribes brought their traditions of biblical interpretation and reports on debates about what observant Jews should and should not do.

Before A.D. 70 the Pharisees took special interest in the observance of Sabbaths and festivals, marriage laws, ritual purity, tithes, rules about raising crops, and other such matters. The Gospels and the Jewish historian Josephus present the Pharisees as a powerful religious movement that sought to extend its traditions to all Israel. The Pharisees' program was not central or dependent on the temple but rather sought to replicate temple spirituality in the home and everyday life, and promoted the ideals of Israel as a priestly people and a holy nation. Thus they could provide a firm religious foundation for an Israel deprived of its temple and political control of the land.

Matthew's Response

Matthew shared the hopes of *4 Ezra* and *2 Baruch*. But he identified the Messiah as Jesus of Nazareth and took Jesus' interpretations of the Law as the proper guide to behavior in the present. He also shared the practical agenda of formative Judaism on many points. But he rejected the Pharisees' traditions and interpretations in favor of Jesus' teachings and example. Thus Matthew's Gospel emerges as a Jewish-Christian response to the events of A.D. 70.

Among the issues of special concern for both the transitioning Jewish community and Matthew the Gospel writer were Sabbath observance, ritual purity, and marriage and divorce.

Sabbath Observance

Matthew 12:1–14 contains two episodes on Sabbath observance. It is likely that Matthew's largely Jewish-Christian community continued to observe the Jewish Sabbath. This is affirmed by Matthew's insertion of the hope that the great tribulation not occur on a Sabbath (24:20), because it might present a crisis of conscience for Jewish Christians.

The first Sabbath episode (12:1–8) deals with the disciples plucking grain on a Sabbath. The Pharisees in Matthew's version sharpen the question in terms of the late first-century Jewish debate: "Look, your disciples are doing what is not lawful to do on the Sabbath." What the disciples were doing could come under the category of reaping, which was in the list of thirty-nine kinds of work forbidden on the Sabbath according to the Mishnah (*Sabbath* 7:2).

In revising Mark's account, Matthew supplies a reason for the disciples' behavior (they were hungry), deletes the mistaken reference to Abiathar as the high priest, adds as another precedent the activity of the priests in the temple on the Sabbath, introduces a typically Jewish mode of argument in 12:6 ("from the light to the heavy"), and provides Hosea 6:6 ("I desire mercy and not sacrifice") as a biblical foundation. He also bypasses the radical saying about the Sabbath having been made for humankind (Mark 2:27).

Thus in Matthew's Gospel, Jesus argues the issue of Sabbath observance in the framework of first-century Judaism and according to the customary modes of Jewish argument and proof.

The second Sabbath episode (12:9–14) concerns healing on the Sabbath. Matthew's version locates the episode in "their synagogue," thus setting it in the context of controversy from the start. The opponents confront Jesus directly with their question: "Is it lawful to cure on the Sabbath?" Jesus' response takes as its starting point a case that was much debated among Jews of the time: whether one could rescue an animal that had fallen into a pit on the Sabbath. The Essenes gave a negative response according to the *Damascus Document* 11:13–14. On this issue the Pharisees were more flexible and liberal than the Essenes. Here Jesus agrees with the Pharisees. His basic principle is that "it is lawful to do good on the Sabbath." The healing of the man with the withered hand gets relegated to second place. Nevertheless, it angers the Pharisees so much that they make plans to destroy Jesus. While they agree with Jesus on rescuing animals on the Sabbath, they regard this healing on the Sabbath as unnecessary and thus unlawful since the man was not in danger of death.

Ritual Purity

Another issue of common concern to Matthew and formative Judaism was ritual purity. The matter is taken up in Mark 7:1–23 where Mark draws some radical conclusions. First, in Mark's version the Pharisees and scribes are accused of neglecting God's Law and holding only to their human traditions. Then in a parenthetical remark (7:19b) Mark infers from Jesus' insistence on the superiority of moral purity over ritual purity that he annulled the biblical purity laws entirely, "Thus he declared all foods clean."

While preserving the framework of Mark 7:1–23, Matthew in 15:1–20 avoids Mark's "radical" conclusion and offers a response to the Pharisees and scribes that was more at home within late first-century Judaism. The opponents' objection to Jesus and his disciples concerns not the Law itself but rather the traditions surrounding the Law: "Why do your disciples break the tradition of the elders? For they do not wash their hands before they eat" (15:2). The biblical basis for washing hands before meals was slight (but see Leviticus 15:11). In fact, it seems to have been just a pious practice. The issue was not personal hygiene but ritual purity.

In Matthew's telling, Jesus first attacks the emphasis of the Pharisees and scribes on their traditions by appealing to the unrelated practice of Qorban, which allowed one to declare something sacred and a gift to God and thus exempt from the claims of others (including one's parents). The point is that the tradition of the scribes and Pharisees can lead to neglect of some very serious biblical commandments such as honoring one's parents. When told that his argument and his emphasis on moral purity had offended the Pharisees, Jesus calls them "blind guides" whose followers will end up in a pit with them. The conclusion to the discussion is clear: "To eat with unwashed hands does not defile a person." Note again that there is no mention of Jesus declaring all foods clean. Thus Matthew's version constitutes a Jewish-Christian response to an issue that was important in formative Judaism and that set the Christians against those who controlled "their synagogues."

Marriage and Divorce

A third issue that helps situate Matthew's Gospel with respect to Judaism appears in the lengthy treatment of marriage and divorce in 19:1–9. In Mark 10:1–2 Jesus is asked, "Is it lawful for a man to divorce his wife?" The biblical legislation about divorce is surprisingly oblique and scanty (see Deuteronomy 24:1–4). But since divorce had long been regarded as acceptable, the questioners in Mark's Gospel seem anxious to place Jesus in the position of contradicting the Torah. Jesus' radical position of "no divorce" (10:9) was apparently well known. There is some evidence that in prohibiting divorce and remarriage, Jesus agreed with the Dead Sea community. His strict teaching appears in the Q saying in Luke 16:18 and in Paul's statement in 1 Corinthians 7:10–11. Mark's Gospel also included the case of a wife divorcing her husband (10:12), something that was very unusual in Judaism.

Matthew took over Mark's basic teaching about marriage—that is, God's original intention in creation was that the two should become "one flesh" (19:5–6) and that Deuteronomy 24:1–4 should be taken as a concession rather than as a command. The three principal changes in 19:1–9, however, reflect Matthew's effort to place Jesus' teaching more squarely in the context of late first-century Judaism. The Pharisees' question in 19:3 ("Is it lawful to divorce one's wife for any cause?") related Jesus' teaching to the contemporary Jewish debate about the grounds for divorce.

The summary of Jesus' teaching in 19:9 ("Whoever divorces his wife, except for unchastity, and marries another commits adultery") modifies the absolute teaching in Mark 10:11 by including an exception. The Greek term *porneia* (see also Matthew 5:31–32) may refer to marriages within degrees of kinship forbidden by Leviticus 18:6–18. But it is more likely that it alludes to the controversy over the enigmatic phrase in Deuteronomy 24:1: "something objectionable." According to Mishnah *Gittin* 9:10, the School of Shammai read it as "something shameful" and interpreted it as sexual misconduct on the wife's part. The School of Hillel and Rabbi Aqiba interpreted it more freely to include the wife's poor cooking or lack of beauty as grounds for divorce by the husband. Here in Matthew's account, Jesus sides with the more conservative School of Shammai. Finally Matthew omits the case of a woman initiating divorce proceedings in Mark 10:12, presumably as not applicable in a Jewish or Jewish-Christian setting.

Controversies

When read as a late first-century Jewish book, Matthew's Gospel fits well in the crisis of Jewish national and religious identity. In this setting its controversy passages are part of a "family quarrel" within Judaism as various groups tried to establish their claims to carry on the tradition of Israel as God's people. But when taken out of this historical context, these texts can become dangerous sources of anti-Judaism.

The most aggressive text is Matthew 23. It begins in 23:1–12 with a severe warning to avoid the religious style of the scribes and Pharisees, especially their public displays of piety in dress, seeking places of honor, and the cultivation of honorific titles such as "rabbi," "teacher," and "father." Then there are seven "woes" (23:13–36) that accuse the scribes and Pharisees of hindering people from entering God's kingdom, harming their converts, splitting hairs regarding oaths, neglecting the major concerns of the Law, and so forth. The scribes and Pharisees emerge as "hypocrites," which is one of Matthew's favorite designations for the opponents of Jesus.

Many of the parables in Matthew's account also carry a controversial element. A major theme in the parables in chapter 13 is the rejection and acceptance of the good news about God's kingdom preached by Jesus. Likewise, the blocks of parables in 21—22 (two sons, tenants, royal marriage feast) and 24—25 (two servants, ten bridesmaids, talents) distinguish those who accept the gospel and are thus prepared for the coming of God's kingdom (Jewish Christians) from those who reject it and are judged severely (the scribes and Pharisees).

In Matthew's account of Jesus' suffering and death, the burden of responsibility for Jesus' death is placed on the Jewish leaders (who goad Pilate into having Jesus executed). However, the cry of the people in Matthew 27:25 ("His blood be on us and on our children!") appears to extend that responsibility to Jews as a collective entity. In Matthew's context, however, the phrase "on our children" may have been limited to a single generation, that of the destruction of Jerusalem and its temple in A.D. 70 and Matthew's Jewish opponents in the late first century. Though understandable in the context of a family quarrel within Judaism of that time, this statement can and has become dangerous when its historical setting is ignored.

As the most "Jewish" of the Gospels, Matthew has historically been a major source for what Christians know (or think they know) about Judaism. From this Gospel there have emerged Christian stereotypes about Jewish legalism, Jewish responsibility for the death of Jesus, and the idea of the Jews as a self-cursed people and killers of God. Matthew is largely responsible for the customary English-language identification of Pharisaism and hypocrisy. At best, Matthew has helped Christians clarify their own identity with regard to Judaism. At worst, Matthew has provided anti-Semites with dangerous ammunition.

For Reflection and Discussion

How does attention to Matthew's historical setting help you understand better why and how he wrote his Gospel?

How does comparing similar texts in Mark help bring out Matthew's distinctive approach to his Jewish heritage?

How would you explain to a Jewish friend Jesus' harsh comments about the scribes and Pharisees in Matthew's Gospel?

And Jesus came and said to them, "All authority in heaven and on earth has been given to me. Go therefore and make disciples of all nations, baptizing them in the name of the Father and of the Son and of the Holy Spirit, and teaching them to obey everything that I have commanded you. And remember, I am with you always, to the end of the age."

—Matthew 28:18–20

9

A Christian Gospel

We can be enlightened by reading Matthew's Gospel as a historical document of late first-century Judaism and early Jewish Christianity. But Christian believers cannot simply leave it in the past. For us, Matthew's work expresses (at least in part) the good news of Jesus Christ for us today. As a "Gospel," it can be classified among those writings that proclaim the story of Jesus the Son of God. As such it is a specific application of the early Christian gospel for certain Jewish Christians in the late first century. But it can be—and is—read with devotion and profit even now, more than nineteen hundred years later by people throughout the world. Matthew's book is not exhausted by reading it in its original setting. In other words, it has become a classic text, one that has transcended the historical circumstances of its original composition.

From what we know about the long and complicated history of the New Testament canon, there was little dispute among the church fathers about Matthew's Gospel being an authoritative Christian book. If Mark was, indeed, the first Gospel written, Matthew's second edition of Mark's Gospel, with his extensive revision and expansion, was so successful that it overshadowed Mark almost entirely. Matthew's Gospel soon became the church's book, exercising such influence and dominance that Augustine viewed Mark as a poor summary of Matthew. Of the three Synoptic Gospels, Matthew dominated the liturgy of the church and influenced theology, especially in Roman Catholic circles.

The lessening of Matthew's dominance in recent years has ironically helped us see more clearly the distinctive achievements of this Evangelist. The widespread acceptance of Matthew's Gospel as a revised and expanded version of Mark has sensitized us to his skill as a transmitter and interpreter of traditions. The insight that the four Gospels should not be harmonized and homogenized but rather viewed as four complementary portraits of Jesus has encouraged readers to look at where and how Matthew differs from the others. The revision of the Catholic Church's lectionary after Vatican II included a three-year cycle of Gospel readings for Sundays: Year A (Matthew), Year B (Mark), and Year C (Luke). Selections from John's Gospel are spread over the three-year cycle, and are especially prominent during Lent and the Easter season. This practice enables us to appreciate better the differences among the Gospels and to look at Jesus from the perspective of one Evangelist over a long period of time. Matthew's Christian theology revolves around several key themes.

The Kingdom of Heaven

In Matthew's Gospel the focus of Jesus' preaching and activity is the kingdom of heaven. The summary of his teaching placed at the beginning of his public ministry makes this clear: "Repent, for the kingdom of heaven is at hand" (4:17). Thus Jesus stands in line with John the Baptist, who, in Matthew's Gospel, says the very same thing (see 3:2). And it prepares us for the petition in the Lord's Prayer, "Thy kingdom come" (6:10).

Hope for the coming kingdom of God in its fullness was characteristic of at least some Jewish groups in Jesus' time. It was the dominant concern in the apocalypses from Daniel to *4 Ezra* and *2 Baruch*, and appears in many of the Dead Sea scrolls. Their hope was that soon God's reign would be so manifest that all creation would acknowledge God as the creator and sovereign lord.

Instead of the more common phrase "kingdom of God," Matthew generally uses the Jewish variant expression—"kingdom of heaven"—as a way of avoiding too frequent and perhaps careless use of the word "God." By prefacing the first block of Jesus' teachings with the Beatitudes (5:3–12), Matthew gives the Sermon on the Mount and everything that follows a future aspect. "Blessed are the poor in spirit, for theirs is the kingdom of heaven." His model prayer (6:9–13) is a plea for the coming of God's kingdom in its fullness and for physical and spiritual sustenance as we wait for it. Jesus' acts of healing in chapters 8 and 9 and his other miracles (see 11:4–5) are signs that God's reign is breaking into human existence. To some extent, especially in Jesus' ministry, the fullness of God's reign has been anticipated or inaugurated. In the parables of chapter 13, Jesus emphasizes that the kingdom is already present; it is a seed, a treasure, or a precious pearl. And the kingdom is a present enough reality to suffer opposition (see 11:12).

Jesus' final discourse in chapters 24 and 25 stresses the future aspects of the full coming of God's kingdom. Its first part (24:1–36) basically reproduces Mark 13:1–37. But the various parables in the second part (24:37—25:30) emphasize the theme of constant vigilance because the precise timing remains uncertain: "You must be ready, for the Son of Man is coming at an hour you do not expect" (24:44). Matthew's treatment of the kingdom highlights Jesus' pivotal role in its coming, its presence in his ministry, and the disciples' need to prepare for it and remain watchful.

Christ

Matthew's most obvious addition to Mark's Gospel is the infancy narrative at the beginning. These stories tell us who Jesus was and where he came from. The genealogy aligns Jesus with Abraham, David, and other major figures in the biblical tradition. Even the unusual mode of his birth in 1:18–25 (virginal conception) is prepared for by including the women Tamar, Rahab, Ruth, and Bathsheba in the genealogy.

Another obvious Matthean emphasis is the use of Old Testament fulfillment quotations ("All this took place to fulfill what the Lord had spoken through the prophet"). The point is that from start to finish, Jesus' life is in perfect harmony with God's will as revealed in the Scriptures. The unusual nature of Jesus' birth and his strange journey as a child all evoke quotations from Scripture (1:23; 2:15, 18, 23). Other fulfillment quotations appear in connection with

- Jesus' ministry in Galilee (4:15–16)
- his healings (8:17)

- his role as God's Servant (12:18–21)
- his use of parables (13:35)
- his entrance into Jerusalem on Palm Sunday (21:5)
- his arrest (26:56)
- and his betrayal by Judas (27:9–10).

Matthew makes use of the common early Christian titles for Jesus: Son of David, Servant of God, Son of God, Messiah, Son of Man, and Lord. But he gives them distinctive twists.

- Jesus as the Son of David is the royal Messiah sent to Israel to heal those who, in the eyes of society, count for nothing (20:29–34).
- Jesus' as God's Servant takes upon himself our infirmities and diseases (8:17; see Isaiah 53:4).
- As the Son of God, Jesus functions as Israel did (or should have done) in the Scriptures (2:15; 3:17; 4:1–11).
- As the Messiah, Jesus is a healer and teacher rather than a military commander and political ruler as the Messiah appears in other Jewish texts of the time.
- As the Son of Man, Jesus is more clearly defined than "the one like a son of man" in Daniel 7:13–14, and his future coming will usher in the resurrection of the dead, the Last Judgment, and the fullness of God's kingdom.
- Jesus as Emmanuel ("God with us," Isaiah 7:14) can be properly addressed as "Lord," thus evincing an element of his divinity.
- Matthew's Jesus is also a wisdom teacher and even Wisdom incarnate (11:25–30).

- And in the passion narrative, Jesus follows the pattern set by Jeremiah, the prophet who suffered for his integrity, in speaking hard truths to the leaders of his people.

The Law

Matthew's Jesus proclaims in 5:17, "Think not that I have come to abolish the Law and the Prophets. I have not come to abolish them but to fulfill them." But in 5:21–48 Jesus could appear as abolishing the biblical commandments about divorce, swearing oaths, retaliation, and hating one's enemies (5:44). Either Matthew (or Jesus) is inconsistent, or we are misunderstanding the text.

The key to understanding Matthew 5:17–48 is identifying the correct definition of fulfillment. If we take seriously Matthew's claim that Jesus came not to abolish but to fulfill the Torah, then fulfillment means going to the root of what the Law and the prophets teach, sharpening their demands, attending to the internal dispositions from which evil actions proceed, and avoiding situations in which the commandments might be broken.

So Matthew's Jesus does not render the biblical commandments obsolete or useless. Rather, he interprets the Law in such a way that leads to its goal and its fullness. The first statement attacks anger as the root of murder, and the second attacks lust as the root of adultery. To avoid the divorce procedure entirely one should avoid divorce itself, and to avoid swearing falsely one should avoid taking oaths entirely. The statement about nonretaliation counsels Jesus' followers to forgo seeking revenge through violence. The final statement urges an inclusive love following God's own example, one that includes even our enemies. Here and elsewhere in Matthew's Gospel Jesus appears as the authoritative interpreter of the Jewish Law. Those who want a sure guide to understanding and practicing the Torah should look to the teachings and example of Jesus. His summary statements about the Golden Rule ("do unto others . . . ," 7:12) and the love commandment regarding God and neighbor (22:34–40) do not invalidate the other biblical precepts. Rather, they offer a perspective or vantage point from which God's will, revealed in the Law and the prophets, may be perceived and practiced. The Law and the prophets as interpreted and practiced by Jesus retain their authority because in Jesus they reach their ultimate purpose.

Ethics

Matthew's Gospel places a strong emphasis on practical action: "Not everyone who says to me 'Lord, Lord' shall enter the kingdom of heaven, but the one who does the will of my Father who is in heaven" (7:21). His is an eminently practical Gospel, retaining the traditional Jewish link between knowing and doing.

The horizon against which the ethical teachings in Matthew are practiced is hope for the coming kingdom of God. Since the precise time of its coming is unknown, the follower of Jesus should be on guard always and live as if the fullness of God's kingdom were to erupt at any moment. Jesus' ethical teaching in Matthew comes from not only the Law and the prophets as interpreted by Jesus but also from the collections of Jesus' wisdom in the five large discourses in chapters 5–7, 10, 13, 18, and 24–25. Among these, the Sermon on the Mount serves as the prime example of Jesus' instructions for God's people gathered around him.

At several points (5:20; 7:21; 18:3; 19:23–24; 21:31–32), Jesus is quite direct about the link between human action and entering God's kingdom. Whoever awaits God's universal reign must express this hope in action, or risk losing out on God's gift of the kingdom. Righteousness (or justice) reigns where the Father's will is realized and Jesus' disciples live in harmony with God's plan and purpose. Righteousness consists in bringing to fullness what was proclaimed by Jesus and begun in his teaching and healing ministry. The faithful disciples of Jesus recognize that in Jesus God has begun to act in a new way. They receive God's directives as people of faith and try to act on them.

Church

Those who gather in Jesus' name (18:20) will enjoy the presence of the risen Lord for all time (28:20), the presence of the one identified as Emmanuel (1:23) or "God with us." The disciples who carry on Jesus' mission of teaching and healing are more than historical figures of the faith but are our primary examples for the church today. They carry on the message of Jesus and show how people can live in conformity with God's will. Whereas in Mark's Gospel the disciples frequently misunderstand Jesus, in Matthew they do generally understand him (see 13:52; 16:12). They sometimes, however, exhibit "little faith" (see 6:30; 8:26; 14:31; 16:8; 17:20)—it is true faith, but it falters and fails at times. By calling Jesus' followers "brothers" and "little ones," Matthew encourages his community (and our faith community today) to identify with Jesus' first followers. We are to avoid titles of honor and use instead "disciple" or "learner." The disciples' task in turn is to "make disciples of all nations" (28:19).

Peter, who often shows "little faith," is our concrete example of how Matthew understood discipleship. Despite his faults, Peter comes to recognize (by divine revelation) who Jesus really is. And through Peter "the rock," the power to bind and loose is given to the whole circle of Jesus' disciples (18:18).

According to Matthew, the followers of Jesus constitute the people of God. Through Jesus the Jew and in response to his command (28:19–20), non-Jews can become part of God's people. The parable of the vineyard (21:33–46) is crucial for understanding the place of the church in salvation history. The vineyard is Israel as God's people (Isaiah 5:1–7), the owner is God, the tenants are Israel's leaders in Jesus' and Matthew's time, the servants are the prophets, and the son is Jesus. The owner of the vineyard (God) "will put those wretches to a miserable death, and let the vineyard to other tenants who will give him the fruits in their seasons" (21:41; see 21:43). Those from whom the vineyard is taken are the Jewish leaders and their allies. Those who "bear fruit" (see 3:8, 10; 7:16–20; 12:33; 13:8) are the faithful followers of Jesus. Matthew very likely interpreted the fall of Jerusalem in A.D. 70 as a just judgment on Israel's (bad) leaders (see 27:25).

For Reflection and Discussion

How might you describe the figure of Jesus as he comes to you through Matthew's Gospel?

What influence, if any, does the biblical theme of "the kingdom of heaven" have on your life?

Try to compose at least one statement describing what the church today might learn from Matthew's Gospel.

PART FOUR

Matthew's Gospel in Christian Life

10

Preaching and Teaching
This Gospel

By understanding Matthew's Gospel as a late-first-century Jewish book, we can better appreciate it as a Christian Gospel. Teachers and preachers might take advantage of the Year of Matthew to learn more about the history of the Jewish people and about Judaism as a living religion today.

Since 1945 there has been an extraordinary burst of scholarly energy and interest in Judaism during the time of Jesus. This enthusiasm has several different roots: 1) efforts to deal with the reality of the Nazi Holocaust of the Jewish community in Europe; 2) the discovery of the Dead Sea scrolls; 3) a growth in historical consciousness; 4) and greater appreciation of how important it is to understand the historical and religious setting in which Jesus lived and worked. Fresh translations of the Old Testament Pseudepigrapha, the Dead Sea scrolls, writings of Philo and Josephus, and the rabbinic writings (Mishnah, Tosefta, Talmuds, Targums) are now available in English. Reliable introductions, handbooks, and scholarly periodicals help us open up the content of these often difficult documents.

Christian preachers and teachers are the main sources that ordinary Catholics have for their knowledge about the Bible and Judaism. In fact, several sociological studies have demonstrated that preachers and teachers bear the most responsibility for perpetuating negative stereotypes and misinformation about Jews and Judaism. In response to Vatican II's *Nostra aetate* 4, Christian preachers and teachers have a special duty to inform themselves and their people about the historical context in which Jesus the Word of God became flesh and dwelt among us. That duty includes learning about first-century Judaism and presenting some of Matthew's statements about the scribes and Pharisees (especially chapter 23) with that environment in mind. It also involves looking more carefully at old stereotypes about Jewish "legalism," Pharisaic "hypocrisy," and the charge of "deicide" against a "self-cursed" people (27:25). For a full treatment of avoiding anti-Judaism in teaching and preaching Matthew, Mark, and Luke, see my *The Synoptic Gospels Set Free: Preaching without Anti-Judaism* (Paulist Press, 2009).

Besides providing an impetus to learn more about Judaism, the Year of Matthew offers the opportunity to look at some timely aspects of Christian theology. Throughout his Gospel, Matthew deals with the relationship between tradition and newness. From the four women present in the genealogy of Jesus (1:1–17) to the risen Lord's command to include Gentiles in his people (28:16–20), Matthew seeks to hold together the riches of the Jewish tradition and the new work that God has accomplished in the person of Jesus. Matthew's ideal is expressed in what many commentators have described as the self-portrait of the Evangelist in 13:52: "Every scribe who has been trained for the kingdom of heaven is like the master of a household who brings out of his treasure what is new and what is old." Some of Matthew's attempts to hold together tradition and newness (for example, his positive attitude toward observing the Torah) may not be convincing to Christians today. But in many respects, Matthew offers a good example to those of us who seek to hold on to what is good and true in the Jewish and early Christian traditions while adapting to the needs and challenges of a fast-changing world.

Many Christians today seek a system of belief that has true continuity between belief and action. Matthew's Gospel is rightly praised as moral and practical. But its noble and challenging teachings (especially those in the Sermon on the Mount) appear in the broader theological context with the full coming of God's kingdom as their horizon, Jesus as the messenger and presence of God among us, and the Christian community as the place where God's version of righteousness or justice can be sought and cultivated. The Matthean Christian seeks to be "perfect" (see 5:48; 19:20) in the biblical sense of the term (which means "whole, undivided") and takes as the model the wholeness of God: "Be perfect, therefore, as your heavenly Father is perfect" (5:48).

Matthew in the Sunday Lectionary for Year A

The lectionary (the book containing the Scripture readings at Masses) used in Catholic and many other Christian churches was developed in response to the directives of Vatican II and promulgated in 1970. Its adoption has greatly expanded our liturgical exposure to both the Old and New Testaments.

The basic principle of the revised lectionary is "continuous" reading. The three-year Sunday cycle emphasizes each Synoptic Gospel in turn: Matthew (Year A), Mark (Year B), and Luke (Year C). For the passages from Matthew's Gospel that appear in the Year A Sunday cycle, see the Appendix on pp. 129–130. Passages from John's Gospel are read during Lent and the Easter season and other important points in the liturgical year. The Old Testament readings have generally been chosen because of some relationship with the Gospel text. The responsorial psalm often serves as a bridge between the first and third readings. The second readings, from Paul's letters or other New Testament epistles, are usually on a separate cycle but often are related thematically to the other texts.

On the weekdays during Ordinary Time in both Year I (odd-numbered years) and II (even-numbered years), there is continuous reading of large segments of Mark (January to early June, interrupted by Lent and the Easter season), Matthew (from early June to early September), and Luke (from early September to Advent). The first reading is taken either from parts of the Old Testament or from the New Testament epistles. The responsorial psalm usually goes with the first reading.

The structure of the current lectionary enables us better to recognize and appreciate the distinctive portraits of Jesus in each Gospel. For Matthew, Jesus is the wise teacher who interprets and adapts what God had revealed to Israel. According to Mark,

Jesus is the suffering Messiah whose teachings and miracles must be placed in the context of the cross. For Luke, Jesus is the best example of his own teachings and one who dies a martyr's death. According to John, Jesus shows us the way to eternal life with his heavenly Father, and his death and resurrection constitute his exaltation and God's victory over death.

Catholic Biblical Interpretation

The Catholic approach to interpreting the Bible respects its historical character and complex origins, as well as its ongoing spiritual significance. For a full treatment, see my *How Do Catholics Read the Bible* (Rowman & Littlefield, 2005).

From the very beginning, the Bible and the church have existed in a kind of circular or symbiotic relationship. The Old Testament shaped the language and thought of Jesus and the first Christians. They in turn produced the books that comprise the New Testament. The church, under the guidance of the Holy Spirit, determined which books belonged in the canon (or authoritative list) of Sacred Scriptures. And the books in the biblical canon have provided the rules and norms for the church's faith and practice throughout the centuries.

In describing what the Bible is, Vatican II's 1965 *Dogmatic Constitution on Divine Revelation (Dei verbum)* 13 used the formula "the words of God in the words of men." Echoing the traditional description of Christ as "true God and true man," this formula seeks to do justice to the Bible's divine and human

aspects. The same document instructs interpreters to attend carefully to the literary conventions and cultural assumptions of
the biblical writers and to interpret the texts accordingly. It also
insists that Scripture be read and interpreted "in the light of the
same Spirit by whom it was written" (12).

With regard to the Gospels, the Council in *Dei verbum* 19
distinguished three stages in their development:

- the actual events of Jesus' life,
- the traditions from and about Jesus that circulated in the
  early churches in oral and written forms,
- and the shaping of these traditions by the Evangelists into
  narratives that also addressed the pastoral needs of their
  communities.

This process occurred from the time of Jesus to the end of the
first century A.D. The Council's statements placed more emphasis
on the role of the Evangelists as transmitters and interpreters of
traditions than as eyewitness reporters.

The hope of Vatican II was that "all the preaching of the
Church, as indeed the entire Christian religion, should be nour-
ished and ruled by Sacred Scripture" (*Dei verbum* 21). The current
lectionary can be (and is) used not only for preaching but also in
religious education, Bible study groups, and personal prayer. For
full treatments of *Lectio divina* and Ignatian contemplation as
ways of reading and praying over biblical texts, see Chapter 10 in
my *Meeting St. Luke Today*.

Matthew in the Sunday Lectionary: Three Examples

For three years (2006–08) I had the privilege of writing "The Word" column in *America* magazine. In the more than 150 essays that I prepared, my goal was to help preachers, teachers, and others who use the lectionary for reflection and prayer to understand better what the biblical readings for each Sunday in the three-year cycle say and mean. The title of each essay and the quotation used as an epigraph pointed out a particular theme that arose from the texts, which was then developed in the essay.

The three examples presented here originally appeared in *America* in 2008. They are not so much sermons or homilies as they are biblical-theological essays intended to break open the biblical texts. In each case the text from Matthew is both important for understanding this Gospel and somewhat difficult to understand. In using these essays it is important to read not only the texts in Matthew's Gospel but also the other biblical texts that accompany it.

Example 1: Just and Merciful (Twenty-Fifth Sunday in Ordinary Time, Cycle A)

Lectionary readings: Isaiah 55:6–9; Psalm 145:2–3, 8–9, 17–18; Philippians 1:20–24, 27; Matthew 20:1–16

Are you envious because I am generous?

—Matthew 20:15

In the Bible, the two great attributes of God are justice and mercy. Today's psalm reminds us that "the Lord is just in all his ways." But we also hear that "the Lord is gracious and merciful," and the reading from Isaiah 55 urges us to "turn to the Lord for mercy; to our God, who is generous in forgiving." Is there any coherence or consistency between these statements about God? Today's parable from Matthew 20, about the generous employer and the various people hired to work in his vineyard, concerns the relationship between God's justice and God's mercy. The point is that while God is both just and merciful, God's mercy can and often does override or trump God's justice.

Jesus lived most of his life in Galilee, the northern part of Israel, where agriculture was (and is) a major occupation. Many workers were hired on a day-to-day basis, in keeping with the employer's needs. During harvest time, landowners needed a lot of help. At other times someone could stand around all day and not be hired. The scene in this parable would have been very familiar to Jesus' first audience.

That a landowner should hire people to work for the day in his vineyard is not surprising. That he should hire them at such different times of the day—dawn, 9 a.m., noon, 3:00 p.m., and 5:00 p.m.—is mildly surprising. But obviously he wants to finish the work that day, and so he keeps on hiring workers. What is startling is that he should pay all the workers the same salary. Those hired late in the day, we can be sure, are pleasantly surprised, and so they marvel at the landowner's generosity. But those hired at dawn become angry and grumble about what they regard as the landowner's injustice. The landowner defends his practice by reminding the grumblers that he has given them what they agreed to—"the usual daily wage" or "what is just" (that is, a denarius). He ends the discussion with a question intended to silence the grumblers, "Are you envious because I am generous?"

One of the persistent complaints against Jesus by his opponents was that he was reaching out to marginal persons, proclaiming to them the mercy of God and promising them entrance into God's kingdom. The tax collectors and sinners were like those hired at 5:00 p.m., whereas the religiously observant (the scribes and Pharisees) were like those hired at dawn. According to the opponents' vision of God's justice, they should receive a greater reward than the latecomers might receive. Indeed, should the latecomers get any reward at all? Should they get the same reward as those who toiled all day? Was Jesus so emphasizing God's mercy that he was neglecting God's justice?

The point of this parable is that eternal life in God's kingdom is a sufficiently abundant reward for everyone. In that respect God is just. And God wants everyone to enjoy that reward. It is never too late; there is always hope, even for latecomers. In that respect God is also merciful.

The parable reminds us that what is at issue here is admission to God's kingdom, and that this is God's gift to give. What those hired early really object to is not the landowner's injustice but rather his generosity. They need to learn that God's kingdom is the favor or grace of God freely given, that the fullness of God's kingdom is enough for everyone, and that each of us will find perfect satisfaction with whatever God may give us.

"For my thoughts are not your thoughts, nor are your ways my ways, says the Lord." These words from the book of Isaiah (55:8) remind us that we should not always judge God according to our limited human perspective of justice. Nor should we always expect God to act according to our human standards and rules. The God revealed in Jesus' life and teaching is both merciful and just. He gives to us all what is due to us. But he is also generous and compassionate to those who need it most. The God who is just in all his ways and holy in all his works is also gracious and merciful, good to all and compassionate toward all his works.

Paul's words from prison ("to me life is Christ, and death is gain," Philippians 1:21) express perfectly the attitude of one who already lives in God's kingdom and whose faith and hope made him fearless in the face of death. Perhaps more than any other biblical writer, Paul understood correctly the mercy of God and its relationship to the justice of God.

Praying with Scripture

Do you want always to judge according to strict justice, or do you want to leave room for mercy? Why do you respond the way you do?

Do you ever feel like the workers who were hired at dawn and had worked all day? If so, what do you do with your resentments?

Have you ever been the recipient of someone's unexpected generosity? If so, how did you respond?

Example 2: God's Vineyard (Twenty-Seventh Sunday in Ordinary Time, Cycle A)

Lectionary readings: Isaiah 5:1–7; Psalm 80:9, 12–16, 19–20; Philippians 4:6–9; Matthew 21:33–43

> The vineyard of the Lord of hosts is the house of Israel.
>
> —Isaiah 5:7

In a vineyard, vines are tended and grapes are picked. In ancient Israel, grapes were a major agricultural product and were used especially for eating and in making wine. At harvest time, vineyards employed many workers. All through the biblical period the vineyard was part of everyday life for many in Israel. So it is not surprising that the vineyard became a biblical symbol for the people of God.

The most famous use of the vineyard symbolism in the Old Testament appears in Isaiah 5, where we are told, "The vineyard of the Lord of hosts is the house of Israel." In his "song" of the vineyard Isaiah recalls the careful and loving treatment that the owner (God) gave to his vineyard (Israel). Nevertheless, the vineyard yielded only wild grapes (sin and rebellion). Out of frustration the owner threatened to destroy the vineyard (by means of the Assyrian army) and make it into a ruin.

The historical context for Isaiah's song of the vineyard was the attack expected against Jerusalem by the Assyrian army in the eighth century B.C. Isaiah foresaw that such an attack would have disastrous effects for Judah, just as an earlier attack had on the northern kingdom of Israel. The only way that this disaster might be averted, according to Isaiah, was for Judah to put aside its sinful and rebellious ways and to try once more to do God's will as the chosen people of God. However, the way in which Isaiah's song of the vineyard is expressed held out little hope for such a conversion.

The vineyard image also appears in today's excerpts from Psalm 80. The psalmist describes Israel's origin as God's people in terms of a vine ("a vine from Egypt you transplanted"), comments on the sorry state of God's vine, and asks God once more to care for and protect his beloved vine. The psalmist very likely had in mind Judah's experience of defeat and exile in the early sixth century B.C. Even though Isaiah's warning had come to pass, the vine remained the object of God's care.

The vineyard image appears also in Jesus' parable in Matthew 21. By this time, the allegory is a familiar one to the Jewish people. The landowner is God; the vineyard is Israel as God's special people; the tenants are the political and religious leaders of Israel; the harvest is the fullness of God's kingdom and the judgment that will accompany it; the servants sent to collect the landowner's produce are the prophets; and the landowner's son is Jesus.

The parable begins by describing God's extraordinary care for the vineyard in terms clearly alluding to Isaiah 5. When the tenants abuse the servants and the son, the owner comes and destroys the wicked tenants. In Matthew's context this is very likely an allusion to the destruction of Jerusalem not only in 587 B.C. but also in A.D. 70. Note, however, that the vineyard itself is preserved and placed under new management. Note also that the chief priests and elders of the people recognize that the parable is being told about them. They need to be replaced as the leaders of God's people.

These three vineyard texts insist that God remains in personal relationship with his people, continues to care for and preserve his people, and stays faithful even when the people fail to do so. Thus the vineyard is an image of hope. It emphasizes God's continuing care for his people. Christians believe that through Jesus' life, death, and resurrection, the people of God have come under new and different leadership from that of the Jewish chief priests and elders. Nevertheless, through Jesus of Nazareth the church retains its historical and organic relationship with Israel as God's people. The problem that Jesus and Matthew had was not with the owner (God) or the vineyard itself (God's people). Rather, it was with the tenants (the leaders). The New Testament parable of the vineyard teaches us to look forward in hope to the fullness of God's kingdom under the guidance of the risen Jesus as Emmanuel, the one who promises to be with us until the end of this age (Matthew 28:20).

In the meantime Paul's advice to the Philippians can help us promote peace on the individual, communal, and international levels. Paul contends that peace of soul is a gift from God, that God's peace surpasses human understanding and that "the God of peace" will be with us. But God's gift of peace needs to be cultivated through prayer, virtuous living, and fidelity to the Gospel.

Praying with Scripture

What are the major similarities and differences between Isaiah's song of the vineyard and Matthew's parable of the vineyard?

How can these vineyard texts contribute to your understanding of the church?

What makes you especially anxious today? How do you deal with your anxieties? How might Paul's advice help you?

Example 3: Render to Caesar? (Twenty-Ninth Sunday in Ordinary Time, Cycle A)

Lectionary readings: Isaiah 45:1, 4–6; Psalm 96:1, 3–5, 7–10; 1 Thessalonians 1:1–5; Matthew 22:15–21

> Then repay to Caesar what belongs to Caesar and to God what belongs to God.
>
> —Matthew 22:21

The saying about rendering to Caesar and to God is often quoted during election years. We may become so accustomed to hearing about rendering to Caesar and to God in modern political contexts that we miss the religious challenge of the biblical text.

The saying comes at the end of a debate in which the Pharisees and the Herodians together confront Jesus. This is not a friendly conversation, since the opponents want to trap Jesus and get him into trouble. The debate is about paying the census tax, which was a tax imposed on Jews as a sign of their subjugation to Rome. Jewish political insurgents (like the Zealots) bitterly resented it. Jewish supporters of the Herod family complied with it and probably embraced it. The Pharisees resented it but went along with it. If Jesus says, "Pay the tax," the insurgents and their supporters will turn against him. If he says, "Don't pay the tax," the Herodians and their allies will report him to the Roman officials, who will in turn arrest him as a revolutionary. The strategy of both groups is to lead him into a trap.

Jesus' basic advice seems to be, "Pay the tax." His reasoning is that, like it or not, Jews had already become a part of the Roman Empire, were integrated into Caesar's economic system, and were using coins marked with Caesar's image and name. Those who use Caesar's coins can hardly object to paying Caesar's tax. But the real emphasis in Jesus' saying comes in the last few words: "Repay to God what belongs to God." With these words, Jesus changes the subject and moves the debate into a different realm. Now the subject is carrying out one's obligations to God. The point is this: If you are so concerned and careful about paying taxes to the state, how much more concerned and careful should you be about the service of God and your obligations to God as your creator and lord.

The biblical writers were mainly concerned with the origin and purpose of political power, not with political structures or policies. They regarded political power as coming from God and as something to be used for the common good. In Romans 13 Paul paints an ideal picture of the Roman Empire and urges the Christians in Rome to be good citizens, cooperate with the imperial officials, and pay their taxes. However, in the book of Revelation, John vehemently criticizes the Roman Empire because apparently some of its local officials in Asia Minor (present-day

Turkey) were forcing Christians to worship the emperor as a god. Jesus' attitude of prudent ambiguity seems to be somewhere between these two extreme views.

In the biblical tradition illustrated by Psalm 96, "the Lord is king." This is one of several psalms that were very likely composed for ancient Israel's annual celebration of the kingship of God. It summons all the people of Israel, all the nations, and all creation to acknowledge and praise God as king of the universe. The psalm celebrates God as the origin of all royal and political power.

The books of the Bible were composed in a world in which human kingship was an almost universal political reality. Among the most powerful and successful rulers in antiquity was the Persian king known as Cyrus the Great. It was Cyrus who conquered Babylon in the sixth century B.C. and allowed the Jewish exiles there to return home and rebuild their temple. Today's reading from Isaiah 45 claims that Cyrus was God's instrument (even though an unwitting one) in freeing Israel's leaders from captivity. The prophet goes so far as to call Cyrus God's "anointed" (or Messiah) and thus traces Cyrus's power to the God of Israel.

In greeting the Thessalonians, Paul refers to Jesus as "the Lord Jesus Christ." Each element in that title had a political overtone. The Roman emperor was called "lord," the name *Jesus* means "savior" and evoked memories of the biblical Joshua, and Christ is the Greek equivalent of the Hebrew "Messiah" and alluded to the reign of the biblical David and the hopes for one of his descendants. Twenty years after Jesus' execution by the Romans, he was being celebrated as sharing divine power with God the Father. That is a remarkable development.

The opening of Paul's letter features the great triad of theological virtues—faith, love, and hope. They have God as their origin and object, and provide a framework not only for Paul's earliest extant letter but also for Christian life as a whole. They can guide us in our efforts at rendering to God what is God's.

Praying With Scripture

How do you react to the biblical concept of the origin and purpose of political power?

Which surprises you more—Cyrus being called the "Messiah" or Jesus being called the "Lord"? How do you think the people of Jesus' day reacted?

In the next election will your religious convictions influence your votes? How and why?

Readings from Matthew's Gospel for the Sundays and Feasts in the Year A

Sundays in Ordinary Time
1. 3:13–17
3. 4:12–23
4. 5:1–12
5. 5:13–16
6. 5:17–37
7. 5:38–48
8. 6:24–34
9. 7:21–27
10. 9:9–13
11. 9:36—10:8
12. 10:26–33
13. 10:37–42
14. 11:25–30
15. 13:1–23
16. 13:24–43
17. 13:44–52
18. 14:13–21
19. 14:22–33
20. 15: 21–28

21. 16:13–20
22. 16:21–27
23. 18:15–20
24. 18:21–35
25. 20:1–16
26. 21:28–32
27. 21:33–43
28. 22:1–14
29. 22:15–21
30. 22:34–40
31. 23:1–12
32. 25:1–13
33. 25:14–30
34. 25:31–46

Advent and Christmas
1. 24:37–44
2. 3:1–12
3. 11:2–11
4. 1:18–24

Christmas: Vigil

1:1–25

Holy Family

2:13–15, 19–23

Epiphany

2:1–12

Lent and Easter

1. 4:1–11
2. 17:1–9

Palm Sunday

26:14—27:66

Easter

28:1–10

For Further Reading

Allison, Dale C. *The Sermon on the Mount: Inspiring the Moral Imagination.* New York: Crossroad, 1999.

Byrne, Brendan. *Lifting the Burden: Reading Matthew's Gospel in the Church Today.* Collegeville: Liturgical Press, 2004.

Davies, William D. and Dale C. Allison. *A Critical and Exegetical Commentary on the Gospel according to Matthew.* 3 vols. Edinburgh: T&T Clark, 1988, 1991, 1997.

Harrington, Daniel J. *The Gospel of Matthew.* Vol. 1, Sacra Pagina. Collegeville: Liturgical Press, 1991; rev. ed., 2007.

Levine, Amy-Jill, and Marianne Blickenstaff, eds. *A Feminist Companion to Matthew.* Cleveland: Pilgrim Press, 2004.

Luz, Ulrich. *Matthew: A Commentary.* 3 vols. Hermeneia. Minneapolis: Fortress, 1989, 2001, 2005.

————. *The Theology of the Gospel of Matthew.* Cambridge— New York: Cambridge University Press, 1995.

Overman, J. Andrew. *Church and Community in Crisis: The Gospel according to Matthew.* Valley Forge, PA: Trinity Press International, 1996.

————. *Matthew's Gospel and Formative Judaism: The Social World of the Matthean Community.* Minneapolis: Fortress, 1990.

Powell, Mark A. *God with Us: A Pastoral Theology of Matthew's Gospel.* Minneapolis: Fortress, 1995.

Saldarini, Anthony J. *Matthew's Christian-Jewish Community.* Chicago: University of Chicago Press, 1994.

Senior, Donald. *Matthew.* Nashville: Abingdon, 1998.

Sim, David C. *The Gospel of Matthew and Christian Judaism: The History and Social Setting of the Matthean Community.* Edinburgh: T&T Clark, 1998.

———and Boris Repschinski, eds. *Matthew and His Christian Contemporaries.* London—New York: T& T Clark, 2008.

Talbert, Charles H. *Reading the Sermon on the Mount: Character Formation and Decision Making in Matthew 5–7.* Columbia: University of South Carolina Press, 2004.

About the Author

Daniel J. Harrington, SJ, is professor of New Testament at Boston College School of Theology and Ministry. He wrote "The Word" column for *America* magazine from 2005 to 2008. He has been writing an annual survey of recent "Books on the Bible" for *America* since 1984. Harrington has been editor of *New Testament Abstracts* since 1972 and served as president of the Catholic Biblical Association in 1985–86. He was a member of the official team for editing the Dead Sea Scrolls and focused on the wisdom texts from Qumran. He is also the editor of the Sacra Pagina commentary on the New Testament (Liturgical Press) to which he contributed the volumes on Matthew, Mark (with John Donahue), and 1 & 2 Peter and Jude (with Donald Senior). He has published extensively on the New Testament and on Second Temple Judaism. He is the author of *Meeting St. Paul Today* (2008) and *Meeting St. Luke Today* (2009), both published by Loyola Press. His *Meeting St. Mark Today* and *Meeting St. John Today* are forthcoming.